OCTOBER 1917 REVOLUTION

A CENTURY LATER

Samir Amin

Published by
Daraja Press
https://darajapress.com

© Samir Amin 2017

All Rights Reserved (unless otherwise specified)

Cover design: Catherine McDonnell based on engraving by P.V. Vasiliye

Editorial Management: Firoze Manji

Library and Archives Canada Cataloguing in Publication
Amin, Samir, author
   October 1917 Revolution : a century later / Samir Amin.
Includes bibliographical references.
Issued in print and electronic formats.
ISBN 978-1-988832-05-0 (softcover).–ISBN 978-1-988832-06-7 (ebook)
   1. Soviet Union–History–Revolution, 1917-1921–
Influence. I. Title.

DK265.9.I5A56 2017   947.084'1   C2017-906029-5

C2017-906030-9

Contents

1. Introduction — 1
2. The October 1917 Revolution began the transformation of the world — 5
3. Reading Capital, reading historical capitalisms — 41
4. Revolutions and counter-revolutions from 1917 to 2017 — 63
5. The sovereign popular project: The alternative to liberal globalization — 83
6. The agrarian question, a century after October 1917 — 107

1.

Introduction

Great revolutions make history. Conservative resistance and counter-revolutions only delay its progress. The French revolution invented modern politics and democracy, the Russian revolution paved the way for the socialist transition, while the Chinese revolution connected the emancipation of peoples oppressed by imperialism with the path to socialism.

These revolutions are great precisely because they are bearers of undertakings that are far ahead of the immediate demands of their time. And that is why they are confronted by the resistance of their times, the origin of the setbacks, "thermidors" and restorations. The ambitions of the great revolutions — expressed in the formulas of the French Revolution (liberty, equality, fraternity), the October Revolution (workers of the world unite), Maoism (workers of the world and all oppressed peoples unite) — do not find resonance in today's reality. But they remain the beacons that illuminate the still unfinished struggles of the peoples for the realization of these goals. It is therefore impossible to understand the contemporary world without understanding these great revolutions.

To commemorate these revolutions, one needs both to assess their ambitions (the utopia of today will be the reality of tomorrow), and to understand the reasons for their temporary setbacks. Conservative and reactionary minds refuse to do so—they wish us to believe that great revolutions have been nothing more than unfortunate accidents, that the peoples who have made them were carried away by deluded enthusiasm, pursuing dead ends that were diversions from the normal current of history. Already on the occasion of the bicentennial of the French

Revolution, the clergy of the media—at the service of reactionary powers—have been deployed to denigrate the French revolution. This year this same media clergy have sought every means to vilify the October revolution. The heirs of the Communism of the Third International are invited to regret the error of their revolutionary convictions of yesteryear. Many in Europe will.

Chapter 1 of this book focuses on the dramatic consequences of the isolation of the October Revolution. I then discuss in Chapter Two the distinction between reading Marx's Capital and the development of the historical realities of the nations of modern capitalism. The former provides the key to understanding capitalism to enable us to comprehend the extent of the break that it represented from all previous societies. The latter allows us precisely to situate, over the long run, these various formations of the contemporary world and thus to assess their unequal capacities to advance along the long road to socialism. Chapter Three offers a reading of how the societies of the contemporary imperialist centre were formed. This can help to explain the grip of the ideology of the conservative order over their peoples, the major obstacle to the release of a creative revolutionary imagination. Chapter Four extends Mao's analysis of the global system from the perspectives of regions in its peripheries. To this end, the chapter presents a strategy of stages of national liberation with possible advances though sovereign and popular national projects. Finally, chapter five returns to the agrarian question, which is at the heart of the challenge facing future advances towards socialism.

This is how I propose to commemorate October 1917, by situating the event in a current context, a context that represents the triumph of the 'liberal' counter-revolution in appearance only, since this system is already advanced on a road of its chaotic decomposition, opening the way to the possible crystallization of a new revolutionary situation.

Samir Amin
Dakar
August 2017

The text of the following chapters first appeared as:

Chapter 1: 'The October 1917 Revolution started off the transformation of the World' *International Critical Thought* (Beijing), vol 7, (2), July 2017,

Chapter 2: 'Reading Capital, reading historical capitalisms.' Monthly Review, Vol 68 (3), July-August 2016

Chapter 3: 'Revolutions and counter revolutions from 1917 to 2017; *Monthly Review*, vol 69, (3), July-Aug 2017

Chapter 4: 'The sovereign popular project, the alternative to liberal globalization' *Journal of Labor and Society*; vol 20, (1), March 2017 .

2.

The October 1917 Revolution began the transformation of the world

The aim of this chapter, written especially for the 100th anniversary of the October 1917 Revolution, is certainly not to denigrate this first gigantic socialist project that echoed the glorious Paris Commune (1871), both of them being parties to the 'storming of the skies'. Humanity owes an enormous debt to the Soviet Union that resulted from this revolution as it was the Red Army, and it alone, that put the Nazi hordes to rout. The model of the Soviet Union, which was a plurinational state based on the support of those both the more and the less destitute, continues to be unequal even today. The support of the Soviet Union to the national liberation struggles of the peoples of Asia and Africa at that time forced the imperialist powers to retreat and to accept a polycentric globalization that was less unequal and more respectful of the sovereignty of nations and of their cultures.

However, neither is the objective of this study to be a nostalgic looking back on this historic event. On the contrary I shall try to identify the mistakes and weaknesses of the original construction and then describe the drift away from it that led to efforts for its reform. And I show how, when these failed and led to the brutal restoration of capitalism, an end was put to this first great wave of humanity's progress towards socialism.

Soviet leaders facing the challenge of history

Lenin, along with the Bolshevik leaders within the old Russian

Workers Social Democratic Party, then Stalin, shaped the history of the October revolution followed by the construction of the USSR. In the following period Khrushchev, Brezhnev and finally Gorbachev and Yeltsin accompanied the decline of that system until its fall. As leaders of revolutionary communist parties and then later as leaders of revolutionary states, the builders were confronted with the problems faced by a triumphant revolution in countries of peripheral capitalism and forced to "revise" (I deliberately use this term, considered sacrilegious by many) the theses inherited from the historical Marxism of the Second International. Lenin and Bukharin went much further than Hobson and Hilferding in their analyses of monopoly capitalism and imperialism and drew this major political conclusion: the imperialist war of 1914-1918 (they were among the few, if not the only ones, to anticipate it) made necessary and possible a revolution led by the proletariat.

With the benefit of hindsight, I will indicate here the limitations of their analyses. Lenin and Bukharin considered imperialism to be a new stage ("the highest") of capitalism associated with the development of monopolies. I question this thesis and contend that historical capitalism has always been imperialist, in the sense that it has led to a polarization between centres and peripheries since its origin (the sixteenth century), which has only increased over the course of its later globalized development. The nineteenth century pre-monopolist system was not less imperialist. Great Britain maintained its hegemony precisely because of its colonial domination of India. Lenin and Bukharin thought that the revolution, begun in Russia ("the weak link"), would continue in the centres (Germany in particular). Their hope was based on an underestimate of the effects of imperialist polarization, which destroyed revolutionary prospects in the centers.

Nevertheless, Lenin quickly learned the necessary historical lesson. The revolution, made in the name of socialism (and communism), was, in fact, something else: mainly a peasant revolution. So what to do? How can the peasantry be linked with the construction of socialism? By making concessions to the market and by respecting newly acquired peasant property; hence by progressing slowly towards socialism? The NEP implemented this strategy.

Yes, but.... Lenin, Bukharin, and Stalin also understood that the imperialist powers would never accept the Revolution or even the NEP. After the hot wars of intervention, the cold war was to become permanent, from 1920 to 1990. Soviet Russia, even though it was far from being able to construct socialism, was able to free itself from the straightjacket that imperialism always strives to impose on all peripheries of the world system that it dominates. In effect, Soviet Russia delinked.

The imperialist West, like the Nazis, could not tolerate the very existence of the Soviet Union. For their part Lenin then Stalin did all they could to reassure the West that they did not intend to 'export' their revolution. They sought peaceful coexistence through all the diplomatic channels available to them.

Between the two world wars Stalin tried desperately to ally the Western democracies against Nazism but the Western powers did not respond to his invitation. On the contrary, they tried to push Hitlerian Germany into making war on the Soviet Union. This was evident, from the tragic 1937 Munich agreement to their refusal to accept the hand that Stalin held out to them.

Fortunately he managed to foil the strategy of the 'democratic' powers by reaching a last-minute agreement with Germany just after the invasion of Poland. Later on, when the United States entered the war, Stalin renewed his attempts to base a durable alliance with Washington and London in the post-war period. He was never to give up. But, again, the coexistence and peace policy pursued by the Soviet Union was defeated by the unilateral decision of Washington and London to end the wartime alliance by initiating the cold war just after the Potsdam agreement, when the United States had the monopoly of nuclear weapons. The United States and their subaltern allies in NATO systematically carried out their 'roll-back' policy from 1946 to 1990, and thereafter. NATO, presented to naïve public opinion as a defensive measure against the aggressive intentions attributed to Moscow, revealed its true nature when it annexed eastern Europe and when this aggressive organization carried out new missions in the Middle East, the Mediterranean, Caucasia, South-East Asia and then Ukraine. (See Geoffrey Roberts, *Stalin's Wars: from World War to Cold War, 1939-1953.*)

So what to do now? Attempt to push for peaceful coexistence, by making concessions if necessary and refraining from intervening too actively on the international stage? But at the same time, it was necessary to be armed to face new and unavoidable attacks. And that implied rapid industrialization, which, in turn, came into conflict with the interests of the peasantry and thus threatened to break the worker- peasant alliance, the foundation of the revolutionary state.

Since 1947, the United States of America, the dominating imperialist power of that epoch, proclaimed the division of the world into two spheres, that of the 'free world' and that of 'communist totalitarianism'. The reality of the Third World was flagrantly ignored: it was felt privileged to belong to the 'free world', as it was 'non-communist'. 'Freedom' was considered as applying only to capital, with complete disregard for the realities of colonial and semi-colonial oppression. The following year Jdanov, in his famous report (in fact, Stalin's), which led to the setting up of the Kominform (an attenuated form of the Third International), also divided the world into two, the socialist sphere (the USSR and Eastern Europe) and the capitalist one (the rest of the world). The report ignored the contradictions within the capitalist sphere which opposed the imperialist centres to the peoples and nations of the peripheries who were engaged in struggles for their liberation.

The Jdanov doctrine pursued one main aim: to impose peaceful coexistence and hence to calm the aggressive passions of the United States and their subaltern European and Japanese allies. In exchange, the Soviet Union would accept a low profile, abstaining from interfering in colonial matters that the imperialist powers considered their internal affairs. The liberation movements, including the Chinese revolution, were not supported with any enthusiasm at that time and they carried on by themselves. But their victory (particularly that of China, of course) was to bring about some changes in international power relationships. Moscow did not perceive this until after Bandung, which enabled it, through its support to the countries in conflict with imperialism, to break out of its isolation and become a major actor in world affairs. In a way, it is not wrong to say that the main change in the world system was the result of this first 'Awakening of the South'. Without this knowledge, the later affirmation of the new 'emerging' powers cannot be understood.

The Jdanov report was accepted without reservation by the European communist parties and of those of Latin America of that era. However, almost immediately it came up against resistance from the communist parties of Asia and the Middle East. This was concealed in the language of that period, for they continued to affirm "the unity of the socialist camp" behind the USSR, but as time went on resistance became more overt with the development of their struggles for regaining independence, particularly after the victory of the Chinese revolution in 1949. To my knowledge, no-one has ever written the history of the formulation of the alternative theory, which gave full rein to the independent initiatives of the countries of Asia and Africa, later to crystallize at Bandung in 1955 and then in the constitution of the Non Aligned Movement (from 1960 defined as Asian-African, plus Cuba). The details are buried in the archives of some communist parties (those of China, India, Indonesia, Egypt, Iraq, Iran and perhaps a few others).

Nevertheless I can bear personal witness to what happened, having been lucky enough, since 1950, to participate in one of the groups of reflection that brought together the Egyptian, Iraqi and Iranian communists and some others. Information about the Chinese debate, inspired by Zhou Enlai was not made known to us by Comrade Wang Hue (the link with the journal *Révolution*, whose editorial committee included myself) until much later, in 1963. We heard echoes of the Indian debate and the split that it had provoked, which was confirmed afterwards by the constitution of the CPM. We knew that debates within the Indonesian and Filipino communist parties developed along the same lines.

It is possible, then, to understand the equivocations of Lenin,

Bukharin, and Stalin. In theoretical terms, there were U-turns from one extreme to the other. Sometimes a determinist attitude inspired by the phased approach inherited from earlier Marxism (first the bourgeois democratic revolution, then the socialist one) predominated, sometimes a voluntarist approach (political action would make it possible to leap over stages). Finally, from 1930-1933, Stalin chose rapid industrialization and armament (and this choice was not without some connection to the rise of fascism).

Collectivization was the price of that choice. Here again we must beware of judging too quickly: all socialists of that period (and even more the capitalists) shared Kautsky's analyses on this point (Kautsky's *Agrarian Question*, published in 1889 was considered as the Bible on that issue by the Second International and even Lenin), and were persuaded that the future belonged to large-scale agriculture. It was a long time before the idea that modernized family farming is more effective than large-scale exploitation was recognized. Agronomists (particularly in France) understood before the economists that the extreme division of labour of the industrial model was inappropriate in agriculture, as the farmer has to deal with the requirements of various tasks that are difficult to anticipate. Anyway the break in the worker-peasant alliance that this choice implied lay behind the abandonment of revolutionary democracy and the autocratic turn.

The Chinese communists appeared later on the revolutionary stage. Mao was able to learn from Bolshevik equivocations. China was confronted with the same problems as Soviet Russia: revolution in a backward country, the necessity of including the peasantry in revolutionary transformation, and the hostility of the imperialist powers. But Mao was able to see more clearly than Lenin, Bukharin, and Stalin. Yes, the Chinese revolution was anti-imperialist and peasant (anti-feudal). But it was not bourgeois democratic; it was popular democratic. The difference is important: the latter type of revolution requires maintaining the worker-peasant alliance over a long period. China was thus able to avoid the fatal error of forced collectivization and invent another way: make all agricultural land state property, give the peasantry equal access to use of this land, and renovate family agriculture.

Mao provided a different response to the agrarian question, based on renewed small-scale family exploitation without private ownership, which reduced the migratory pressure towards the towns. This made it possible to associate the strategic aim of food sovereignty with the construction of a complete and modernized national industrial system. As for a general treatment of the agrarian question, see Chapter 5 of my book *Ending the Crisis of Capitalism or Ending Capitalism?* This formula is certainly the only possible response to the agrarian question in all the countries of the contemporary Global South, although the political conditions required for implementing it have occurred only in China and Vietnam.

Thirty years of critique of Sovietism

– 1 –

Except for individuals with a natural disposition to prophesy, nobody can pretend not to have been somewhat taken aback by the sudden and total collapse of the political systems of Eastern Europe and the USSR. Now that the surprise factor is gone, it is useful to look back at the analyses of these systems that were produced some thirty years before the final fall. At the risk of sounding pretentious, I may say that since 1960 I have been part of a small current on the left that had broadly foreseen what came to a climax between 1989 and 1991. Of course, the collapse we thought highly likely was not the only possible outcome of the crisis of the Soviet system. I do not believe in any unfailing linear determinism in history. The contradictions running through every society always find their resolution in diverse responses according to their class content. It was always possible that the Soviet regime might fall to the right (as happened) or evolve (or fall) to the left. The latter possibility has been ruled out for the immediate future but remains on the agenda of history, not only because there is never an end to history but also because I doubt that the right-wing solution in the making will stabilize the societies of the East, even in the medium term.

The period following Stalin's death in 1953, and especially from the Twentieth Congress in 1956 to the fall of Khrushchev in 1964, was marked by a first attempt claiming to recover from Stalinism and by the open ideological and political dispute between Moscow and Beijing. The next period of so-called Brezhnev glaciation (immobilist strategy) lasted until the arrival of Gorbachev in 1985. Gorbachev's attempt at perestroika after 1985 ended within a few years in the collapse from 1989 to 1991.

The evolutions and successive phases had to be articulated on those operating at a world level. This meant capitalist expansion and the building of the European Union. It meant military balances between the two superpowers and political responses in the arms race. In the Brezhnev period, it meant Soviet initiatives toward the Third World and conflict with China on the one hand, and U.S. Cold War strategies, including Star Wars preparations after 1980, on the other. Internal options and international policies were intertwined during these thirty years.

After 1960, certainly, and even after 1957, I ceased to consider Soviet society as socialist or that the power of the workers was "deformed by bureaucracy," in the famous Trotskyist expression. I had from the beginning regarded the ruling exploiting class (and I do mean class) as a bourgeoisie. This class, the nomenklatura, saw itself in the mirror of West it aspired to replicate. This is what Mao had perfectly expressed when he was addressing cadres of the Chinese Communist Party in 1963: "You [meaning the Chinese party cadres like those of the USSR] have constructed a bourgeoisie. Do not forget: the bourgeoisie does not want socialism, it wants capitalism."

I drew the logical conclusions from this analysis of the Party and the attitude of the masses toward the authorities. To me it was obvious that the masses did not recognize themselves in the authorities, although they continued to proclaim themselves socialist, but they saw them, rather, as their true social adversaries—and rightly so. In these circumstances, the Party was a long-moldering corpse that had become an instrument of social control over the masses exercised by the exploiting ruling class. The Communist Party, crowning the work of the repressive institutions such as the KGB, organized a network of clients among the people, through control and distribution of all social benefits, even the slightest, thus paralyzing their potential revolt.

This kind of party in no way differs from the many one-party systems in the Third World that play the same role (such as Nasserism, the Algerian FLN, the Ba'ath, and the long train of parties in office in Mali, Guinea, Ghana, Tanzania, and others, all who fall under the label of radical nationalism, or in countries, such as the Ivory Coast, who openly opt for capitalism). It is a general pattern suitable for situations where the emergent bourgeoisie has not yet established its ideological hegemony ("the ideology of the ruling class is the dominant ideology in society," said Marx about mature capitalism) and does not appear to exercise legitimate power (this would require a consensus established by the society's adherence to the ideology of its ruling class).

This kind of exercise of power, which fragments the masses through clientship, has a depoliticizing effect, the harm of which should not be underestimated. Events have now shown that in the USSR the depoliticization was of such breadth that the masses believe that the regime they are rid of was socialist, and they ingenuously accept that capitalism is better.

All the elements of the system collapsed like a house of cards as soon as the leaders lost state power. Nobody was prepared to risk their lives to defend an apparatus of this kind. That is why struggles at the top in this kind of party always take the form of palace revolutions, with the grassroots unfailingly accepting those who become winners

I shall not repeat the reasons that made me refuse to believe that fundamental principles of socialism were being implemented, as I have explained them many times. For me, socialism means more than the abolition of private property (a negative characteristic); it has a positive meaning of alternative labor relations other than those defining wage status and alternative social relations allowing society as a whole (and not an apparatus functioning on its behalf) to control its social future. This in turn means a democracy far more advanced than the best bourgeois democracy. In none of these ways was Soviet society different from industrial bourgeois society, and when it moved away from its original goals, it was worse, as its autocratic practice brought it closer to the prevailing model in the areas of peripheral capitalism.

I refused to describe the USSR as capitalist, although its ruling class was in my view bourgeois. My argument was that capitalism means the dispersal of the property of capital as the basis of competition and that state centralization of this property commands a different logic of accumulation. At the political level, I argue that the 1917 revolution was not a bourgeois revolution because of the character of the social forces that were its authors and because of the ideology and social project of its leading forces. This is no average consideration.

I do not attach much significance to a positive description of the system. I have used various terms such as "state capitalism" and "state monopoly capitalism," whose ambiguities I criticized, and finished up with the neutral term "Soviet mode of production." What seemed more important to me was the question of the origins, formation, and evolution of the system and, within this framework, its future.

I was not one of those who always regretted the 1917 revolution. ("It did not have to happen, because the objective conditions for the building of socialism did not exist; it was necessary to stop at the bourgeois revolution"). In my view, the worldwide expansion of capitalism is polarizing, and it is inevitable that the people who are its victims—on the periphery of the system—should revolt against its consequences. One can only support the people in their revolt. To stop at the bourgeois revolution is to betray those peoples, since the necessarily peripheral capitalism that would follow does not provide acceptable responses to the problems that motivated the revolt.

The Russian and Chinese revolutions opened a long transition, the outcome of which is unknown. The dynamic of their evolution may lead to capitalism (and in my view to a peripheral form of it, not similar to what it is in the dominant centers) and both within the society and on a world scale it may encourage progress toward socialism. What is important is to analyze the objective direction of the advance toward socialism. Along with a minority of the communist left, I continue to support the two theses that seemed to me important in analyzing Soviet evolution:

- Collectivization as implemented by Stalin after 1930 broke the worker-peasant alliance of 1917 and, by reinforcing the state's autocratic apparatus, opened the way to the formation of a "new class": the Soviet state bourgeoisie.

- Because of some of its own historical limitations, Leninism had unwittingly prepared the groundwork for this fatal choice. I mean that Leninism had not broken radically with the economism of the Second International (of the Western labour movement, it must be said): its concept of the social neutrality of technology is evidence of this.

Such a society embarking on a long transition faces contradictory demands. On the one hand, it must catch up, in the plain and simple sense of developing the productive forces. On the other hand, in its tendency toward socialism a society in transition offers the alternative of building a society free of economic alienation. The latter characteristically sacrifices the two sources of wealth: the human being reduced to labor power and nature regarded as the inexhaustible object of human exploitation. Can it be done? I always thought the answer was yes, but with great difficulty: a pragmatic compromise to move gradually in the promising direction of the alternative. The economism of Leninism contained the seed of a choice that would gradually make the goal of catching up triumph over the goal of the alternative.

My early adherence to Maoism and to the Cultural Revolution, which I do not repudiate, stems from this analysis. (I was astonished that Lenin had been surprised by Kautsky's betrayal in 1914.) I supported the thesis that Mao established a genuine return to a Marxism that had been distorted by the Western labour movement (and imperialism has its share of responsibility in this drift) even before it was distorted, as it still is, partly, by Leninism.

Maoism offered a critique of Stalinism from the left, while Khrushchev made one from the right. Khrushchev was saying that insufficient concessions have been made to the economic constraints in the technological and scientific revolution, globalization, and the political implications of giving more authority to the enterprise directors, namely the Soviet bourgeoisie. Khrushchev was saying that in these circumstances we would catch up more quickly. Mao was saying that at every step the final goal must be remembered. This was the real meaning of "putting politics in command" (a meaning that has nothing to do with the facile accusation of voluntarism). To avoid losing sight of the final goal, Maoism insisted on equality between workers and peasants (essential in China, but equally so in the Russia of 1930) in order to strengthen their alliance. I explained the goal in terms of what law of value to implement: (i) to surrender to that governing worldwide capitalism and accept thereby peripheral capitalist development; (ii) to envisage building an autocentric national economy, delinked from the world system but analogous to that of advanced capital (the law of value governing the Soviet statist mode of production and creating a Soviet national bourgeoisie); or (iii) to establish relations between the masses based on the law of value of the socialist transition. Mao rightly believed, as later evolution in the USSR and China showed, that the question should be handled at the level of power: challenge the monopoly of the Communist Party, crucible of the new bourgeoisie. Hence the big-character poster launching the Cultural Revolution: "Bombard the Headquarters" (of the Communist Party). Was he wrong to believe that it was the only way to increase workers' control over society and to drive the bureaucracy into retreat? He did not believe that concessions to market laws—more power to directors of enterprises, more competition among enterprises—would advance the people's social power. Was he wrong? I am not saying that concessions should not be made to the market. The New Economic Policy had done this successfully in its time. It had to be done, and more bravely than it was, but there were other conditions. Concessions had to be accompanied by political democratization. The genuine powers of the workers had to be strengthened in this democracy against those of the bourgeois technocrats. The market had to be incorporated into a state policy strongly based on the law of value of the transition to socialism.

The Yugoslavs tried badly and too timidly: too great an opening was made to the exterior; the concessions were too great, worsening internal tendencies to inequality between the republics in the name of competitiveness; and excessive decentralization left the self-managed collectives in a situation of mutual competition. In the USSR, nothing had been done in this direction.

– 2 –

The central issue concerning the Soviet mode of production was whether it was an unstable solution, characteristic of a transitional period that was evolving toward capitalism or socialism, or a new and stable mode that, despite its faults, indicated the future of other normal capitalist societies. I offer a self-criticism on this point. I thought at one time, from 1975 to 1985, that the Soviet mode was a stable and advanced form of what the normal tendency of capital should engender elsewhere, by the very act of centralization of capital, leading from private monopoly to state monopoly. There were signs of this at the time. I am not referring to the apparent stability of Brezhnev's USSR. I am referring rather to the earlier theoreticians (Bukharin's theory on state monopoly capitalism) or to propositions of the time: the convergence of systems that Jan Tinbergen detected, bringing together not only the USSR and the advanced West, but also the positions taken by the left-wing social democracies (in Sweden, for example, with the plan for trade unions to buy up industry) and Eurocommunism. It seemed that statist centralization of capital, by suppressing competition and the opacity of the market, produced similarity in the prices charged by the monopolies and those charged by Gosplan. This parallel evolution inaugurated a return to the dominance of ideology. This ideology was not a return to the metaphysical religions of the tributary age, but the ideology of triumphant commoditization. There was the strong image of George Orwell's *1984* (to whose revived reputation I contributed at the time) and the analysis of the monolithic consensus in the supposedly liberal and democratic societies of the West in Herbert Marcuse's *One-Dimensional Man* that reminded me of my reading of Karl Polanyi. Why couldn't the statist mode be the highest form of capitalism? The Soviet mode foretold a grim future, despite its primitive shape. (How happy Stalin would have been to have the CNN rather than the newspaper *Pravda* to mold a monolithic public opinion, as was done during the Gulf War!). I added the observation that in the bourgeois revolution the struggle of the peasants against the feudalists did not end in the victory of the oppressed but in the rise of a third party: the bourgeoisie. Why should the battle of the workers (or wage earners) against the capitalists not become the business of the "new class"? Events proved me wrong. The Soviet regime proved to be unstable, and the offensive of the worldwide right from 1980 was in the opposite direction: deregulation and privatization had their heyday.

I return to my self-criticism with a subtle distinction. Never mind that the Soviet model was incapable of becoming a definite alternative to be gradually copied by others. Events have shown that it was not. This may reflect only its own weaknesses. It does not mean that in other parts of the developed world, once the recent wave of liberal utopia is over, evolution may not follow a path mapped out by the old USSR.

An assessment is needed of the Soviet cycle now that it is completed. It is not positive overall, or negative. The USSR, and subsequently China and even the countries of Eastern Europe, has built modern autocentric economies such as no country of peripheral capitalism has succeeded in doing. According to my analysis, this is because the Soviet bourgeoisie was produced by a popular, national, and so-called socialist revolution, whereas the bourgeoisies of the Third World, established in the wake of the worldwide expansion of capitalism, are generally of a comprador nature.

It is important to recall the exceptional nature of the construction of the Soviet Union, initiated by Lenin and completed by Stalin. Lenin, the international communist, could not imagine anything but a union of nations working together on an equal basis to construct a common socialism. The Soviet Union, which has never lost sight of this principle, was in fact a plurinational state and not an empire constituted by a metropolis and its colonies.

The Soviet economic system (whether it was socialist or something else) was perfectly integrated: wages and prices were rigorously identical from Moscow to Baku or Tashkent. This has never been the case in the empires of capitalist imperialism (what? the same wage for a British worker and one from Mumbai?). Thus the flow of capital in the Soviet Union went from the advanced regions to the poor peripheries, which was simply the contrary to what happens in the capitalist world. The Soviet Union invented 'international assistance' and genuinely put the principle into practice, while the Western discourse on international assistance is deceptive, accompanied as it is by the pillage of the resources of the dominated peripheries and the gross exploitation of labour.

Thus the destruction of the Union has in no way constituted progress, enabling the so-called oppressed nations to free themselves from the Russian colonial yoke, as the imperial media continue to repeat. Many of the nations, particularly in Central Asia, did not want to leave the Union, from which Yeltsin chased them away with the tacit agreement of his accomplice Gorbachev. Elsewhere—in the Baltic countries, Ukraine and Georgia—the NATO powers openly supported nazi groups and criminal mafiosi to attain their ends (concerning the euro-nazi coup d'état of Kiev, I recommend the reader to my book *Russia and the long Transition from Capitalism to Socialism*, Chapter 6). The people of Eastern Germany were brutally dispossessed of their wealth for the exclusive benefit of a handful of financial oligarchs in Western Germany. A similar destiny has befallen the Greek people, whose wealth has been confiscated for the benefit of the oligarchs of Western Europe. And, in spite of their formal integration into the

European Union, the countries in Eastern Europe have become semi-colonies of their Western partners, particularly Germany. The relationship of Eastern Europe with Western Europe is analogous to that by which Latin America was subordinated by the USA. Today the overt capitalist option of the USSR and Eastern Europe returns to the agenda the peripheralization of their economy and society for which the popular classes (and even the local bourgeoisie) are unprepared because of the depoliticization wrought by blind statist despotism.

– 3 –

I have always refused to treat the specific crisis in the Soviet mode alongside the totally different crises of capitalism. I have also rejected those analyses of the system offered by the capitalist propaganda machinery and vulgarized in the media.

- The distinction between an economy of poverty—socialism—and an economy of abundance—capitalism—leads to an empty ideological discourse. It is obvious that the poverty shown in long lines, for example, was produced by the voluntary freezing of prices, which permitted broad access to consumer goods, which was a concession to egalitarian pressures from the masses and the middle strata. It is obvious that if prices rise massively, there are no more lines, but the seemingly vanished poverty is still there for those who no longer have access to consumer goods. The shops in Mexico and Egypt are packed with goods, and there are no lines in front of the butchers' shops, but meat consumption per head is a third of what it was in Eastern Europe. This childish argument has made a fortune for the Hungarian J. Kornai, who is promoted by the World Bank.

- The command economy, as compared to the self-regulating economy made fashionable by U.S. academics, is also an outrageous simplification. The real Soviet economy was always based on a mixture of adjustments by the market operating outside the plan and administrative orders, especially on investment. The market idealized by the prevailing liberal ideology has never been self-regulating beyond the constraints of the social system where it operates and the state policies that determine its framework. The real problem is that accumulation in the framework of statist centralization of capital (corresponding to an integrated state-class) differs from capitalist accumulation, which in the modern age results not from market laws defined in an ideal abstract but from competition among monopolies.

- From as early as 1935, the priority of the economic apparatus shifted to military expenditure. Does this mean that the Soviet system is military? It is suggested by some that it has a natural expansionism through conquest. Similarly, Jean Jaurès posited that "capitalism bears war within itself like the cloud the storm." This is ideological nonsense. Analysis of the relative significance, and social burden, of military expenditure cannot be conducted purely on the grounds of modes of production. Military expenditure should be analyzed from the structure and conjuncture of national or local and international or regional global systems. From this viewpoint, it is obvious that the arms race was imposed on the USSR by its real enemies and false friends among the capitalist powers.

- The discourse on "totalitarianism" lacks coherence. It has pretentious academic forms in the style of Hannah Arendt or childish forms in the media. A U.S. president used the phrase "Evil Empire" to describe the U.S.'s adversary and came close to the kind of language used by Iran's Ayatollah Khomeini. Was it forgotten that a society grown amorphous would never be able to rid itself of despotism?

I saw in Sovietism an attempt to escape the impasse of Stalinism by going to the right rather than the left. The proposals illustrated what I called "the utopia of constructing a capitalism without capitalists." The Novosibirsk School, which most influenced Gorbachev, pushed the logic of Léon Walras to the limit. It imagined a pure and perfect self-regulating market. As Walras had understood, and Enrico Barone had been explaining since 1908, this did not call for dispersed private property but for total statist centralization of property. Proponents of the Novosibirsk School called for the constant bidding for access to means of production by all individuals who were free to sell their labor or organize production as entrepreneurs. The old dream of Saint-Simon, the scientific management of society taken up by German social democracy (Engels was the first to see it as the dream of capitalism without capitalists), expresses the economistic alienation of all bourgeois ideology, whose unreal and utopian character was shown by historical materialism.

This philosophy is the key to the reformist vision of Khrushchev and Gorbachev and even the adulterated version of the Brezhnev period. History has shown that these concepts were untenable and that the drift to the right would reach its goal in the transformation of the Soviet bourgeoisie into a normal, private property-owning bourgeoisie.

The revolution of the years from 1989 to 1991 was top-down from the ruling class and not bottom-up from the people. The Western media would like to present the revolutions in the East as blows for freedom; they neglect to analyze the vulnerability of democratization, which may very well be only a means of ensuring a transition to crude capitalism, a system that is always despotic, as can be seen from the historical experience of the capitalist peripheries. I disagree. The revolutions can be considered blows for freedom only if the system was overtaken by the left. In their present form, these movements were no more than prodigious and unexpected accelerations of the natural evolution of the system, despite the thesis of totalitarian blockage.

May be Gorbachev thought he could control the reform process and did not expect to be dumped by the majority of the nomenklatura class he represented (as Boris Yeltsin's rise showed), any more than he expected the irrelevance of the Communist Party, which proved to be useless for transmitting the project to the popular level. The Soviet nomenklatura bourgeoisie will be the bourgeoisie of tomorrow, directly appropriating the means of production into private hands and no longer collectively through the intermediary of the state. This is not a social revolution but a political upheaval so vast that it requires radical change among the leadership. It was difficult to avoid the sudden political fragmentation of the former nomenklatura and the manipulation of the national aspirations of the peoples of the former Soviet Union. This is, of course, the business of the Western powers. They will easily take advantage of the situation through the blackmail of financial aid. They will push the frontiers of Russia back to those of sixteenth-century Muscovy and demolish any hope for the country to be a significant competitor on the world scene.

The new oligarchy that was established by Yeltsin and Gorbachev controls Russia's productive system proceeds towards the same transformation of a capitalism of contemporary monopolies which has enabled the economic and political powers to be taken over by the oligarchies that govern alone in the United States, Western Europe and Japan. But while they disposed of States that are at their exclusive service; the power of the oligarchies outside the imperialist triad are only accepted and supported by Washington to the extent that they agree to fulfil their functions of transmission belts for foreign imperialist domination.

The cold war continues in spite of the restoration of capitalism in Russia, the only reason being that the Russian State, having been taken in hand by Putin, does not accept the status

of the dominated power that the United States succeeded in imposing on it during the years of the Yeltsin presidency. And that has happened in spite of the fact that Russia's economic system remains to this day dominated by an oligarchy that would accept without much resistance the status of a dominant comprador class subjected to the requirements of the existing imperialist globalization. The conflict between this class and the ambitions of Putin to reconstruct an independent form of State capitalism is thus bound to increase. From the pursuit of the cold war against Russia it should be understood that the aim of Washington and its subaltern allies in Europe is quite simply to impose on the whole world—and for the exclusive benefit of the USA/Western Europe/Japan—the status of dominated periphery.

– 5 –

For the USSR, as for any other historical society, the external political options were closely linked to the demands of the internal social dynamic. Not for a moment since 1917 have the fascist and democratic Western powers abandoned the idea of defeating the Soviet Union. Despite the USSR's decisive role in defeating the Axis powers, it emerged exhausted from World War II and was threatened by the United States' nuclear monopoly. The Yalta agreements were not a division of the world between victorious imperialisms but a minimum guarantee the Soviet Union had won for its own security.

The Soviet Union, like China, Vietnam, or Cuba, has never sought to export revolution but has on the contrary always practiced prudent diplomacy, with the primary purpose of defending its own state. All the revolutions were conducted virtually against the will of Big Brother: China against the advice of Moscow, and Vietnam and Cuba acting on their own. This fact never shocked me, and I tried to fathom the reasons, without accepting that revolutionaries must submit to the dictates of the Soviet Union. Revolutionaries should rather go further and be self-reliant. Successful revolutionaries have done this (as seen in China, Vietnam, Cuba,).

The second Cold War (after that of the inter war period) was Washington's initiative after 1947. The USSR stuck rigidly to the division at Yalta (hence its attitude to the revolution in Greece), and never in its history did it nurture a project to invade Western Europe. Talk of Soviet bellicosity is pure Western propaganda. The Zhdanov doctrine of a world divided into two camps was characteristically defensive (justifying the nonintervention of the USSR beyond the Yalta boundaries) and inaugurated a period of Western isolation of the USSR, and of China, after 1949. The Atlantic powers never once ceased interfering in the Third World with colonial wars, Israeli aggression, and so on.

The USSR and China began to leave their isolation after the 1955 Bandung Conference, when they saw the advantage they could gain from giving support, albeit limited, to Third World liberation movements. The belated Soviet military effort after 1970 contributed to a genuine balance of deterrence. Then, but only then, did the USSR become a superpower and a new era began. The bipolarity of the twenty years before the Soviet collapse of 1989-1991 is asymmetrical in that the USSR was a superpower only in military terms and was not able to compete with the Western imperialists in their capacity for economic intervention. There was never any symmetry between the actions of the two superpowers and their impact. The United States, with Europe and Japan in the background, pursued a diplomacy of clear goals and familiar methods to ensure domination of the periphery (access to raw materials, markets, military bases, and so on). The United States established hegemony through this shared strategy, and when U.S. economic advantage over its allies began to erode, it used this strategy to maintain its declining hegemony (the Gulf War is the most recent episode).

The goals of Soviet intervention beyond the Yalta boundaries are more difficult to identify.

I did not see Soviet interventions as an aggressive determination to export revolution and to dominate, but rather as a defensive posture from comparative weakness despite the acquisition of parity in nuclear deterrence. The interventions have sometimes been perceived as a manifestation of growing strength. This requires consideration of the debate on "social imperialism," a term devised by the Chinese in 1963. It was a plan for a social compromise between the Soviet bourgeoisie and its people, a revisionist compromise. It was, after all, similar to the social democratic compromise in the West and would have allowed external expansion similar to the colonial expansion supported by the imperialist consensus in the West. There was nothing startling or unimaginable in the concept. The real issue was not whether the Soviet bourgeoisie did or did not want to embark on it but whether it was capable of it. I think the answer to this remains open.

From Lenin to Gorbachev: Enormous advances, followed by dramatic reversals

Progress on the long road to socialism involves the implementation of a planning that gradually substitutes the management of the private economy by the market. The new social ownership of the means of production makes this necessary.

This declaration of principle of course does not solve the question of what forms of planning are appropriate—forms meeting the requirements of that particular stage on that long road. These will be very different if the departure point is that of the advanced capitalist economy (on the hypothesis of a revolutionary advance in the United States or in Western Europe) of that of an economy that is peripheral in the world system (as were those in Russia and China). But whatever the case I do not think it is possible to imagine in advance a Plan that is technically perfect, one that is immediately more effective than the private management of the markets and, on top of that, that enables socialization. The transition will take a long, perhaps a very long time—even a century? This is because the new society being constructed will emerge from the putrid entrails of capitalism, as Marx had already understood and proclaimed.

Moreover, in this gradual advance in social planning (and not just economic) each phase must facilitate the progressive socialization of economic management, that is to say, reinforce—without any interruption—its control by the workers themselves with their power taking over that of the capitalist entrepreneurs. Here again there is no ready-made formula for this fundamental requirement. The direct intervention of the workers at all levels, from the factory to the national, has to be invented by political action as it goes along. Neither the self-management of the enterprise nor the authoritarian planning of the national State are sufficient responses to the challenge, even though elements of both will be part of the system set up to move along the road to socialism.

As things stand at present, the inescapable departure point is the nationalization/State control of the ownership of the main means of production. But this negative definition (abolition of private property) is the only condition that will enable the gradual socialization of the new ownership by the workers.

For example, I myself have proposed the concrete forms that the beginning of this socialization could take in an advanced modern industrial economy and described these forms for an institutionalization of a social regulation of the market. (See my book *The Implosion of Contemporary Capitalism*, pp 123-128.) The criterion for assessing any socialist planning, at each stage of its development, must be: does it advance the socialization of the management of economic, social and political life? Soviet (or Chinese) planning must be measured in light of this criterion.

In fact, the principle of planning was proclaimed by Lenin immediately after the October Revolution and the Gosplan was created in 1921. However its implementation was delayed by the NEP in which agriculture was largely controlled by the better-off peasants (kulaks) to enable the acceleration of the necessary development of industry. Genuine Soviet planning thus only got going with the collectivization that put an end to the NEP—that is, the first Five Year Plan (1929-1933).

I shall not elaborate more on what I have already written above about:

1. The objectives of this planning (described as Stalinist)—in other words the prodigiously rapid industrialization, the priority given to heavy industry and the modernization of armaments;

2. The economic strategy implemented to service this —in other words the transfer of the agricultural surplus (and sometimes more than this) to benefit an extensive industrial accumulation, based on the transfer of large sections of the rural population to constitute an urban working class;

3. The form of this centralized planning, managed authoritatively by the State alone.

The extent to which this adventure can be described as socialist is arguable. There was no alternative to the choice of its objectives if one had to imagine what forms of implementation that would make it possible to advance its socialized management. It was the success of this option that turned the Soviet Union into a new great industrial and military power in 1941 and thus enabled the Red Army—alone—to defeat the Nazis. The victory was in fact won by this army on its own: the support that the West claimed to have provided was limited to a few, insignificant deliveries. And the objective of the military support of the United States and Great Britain—the second front that was initiated by the Normandy landing in 1944—was to prevent the Soviet Union from liberating the whole of Europe by itself.

This is not to deny the admirable courage of the British people who were the only ones not to capitulate in 1940. Nor the courage of the peoples of Yugoslavia and Greece who confronted the nazi invasion by a continual war of liberation. But it does question recognition of the role of the United States that only became mobilized when Nazism was already on the way to being defeated.

The alternative to 'Stalinism' was proposed by Trotsky as from 1927 to 1930: would it have been able to do 'better'? Certainly not, on the contrary. The choices that Trotsky would have made if he had been in charge of the Party and the State (which, in my view, was fortunately excluded) would have led the Soviet Union to certain defeat and enabled the success of the nazi project. Trotsky cherished the myth of a revolutionary European working class (and particularly a German one). He had not learnt the lesson of the failure of the German revolution in 1919-1921: socialism had to progress in only one country, isolated and fought by all the Western powers, as Lenin and Stalin had then understood. Trotsky's projects are now known, having been established not only from the Soviet archives but also from those of Nazi Germany and conservative Great Britain. Gover Furr has provided the proof in minute detail (see *Trotsky's 'Amalgams'*): Trotsky preached 'revolutionary defeatism' (as it could be envisaged in 1914). The defeat of the Red Army would, according to him, have triggered a German anti-nazi revolution!

It was easy for Trotsky an exile as from 1927 and no longer with any responsibilities on the Soviet ship, to repeat untiringly the sacred principles of socialism. From the beginning the Fourth International succumbed to the myth of the world revolution that would be set on the right path by the working classes of the developed capitalist countries. This discourse could be convenient for certain academic Marxists who could afford the luxury of proclaiming their attachment to principles without worrying about being effective in transforming reality. For this reason the Fourth International never left its intellectual ghetto. Of course there were some great exceptions of Marxist intellectuals who, without having responsibilities in running revolutionary parties, still less the State (like Baran, Sweezy, Hobsbawn and others), nevertheless attentively studied the challenges that the historic socialisms had to confront.

Following the same method in the post-war period made it possible to reconstruct, in record time, a country that had been ravaged like none other and even to modernize its military arsenal (nuclear arms and rockets, preparing the success of sputnik). But at the same time these planning methods lost their effectiveness as the economy became more complex. The aims of the Stalinist Plan were drawn up in a very rudimentary way (tons of steel, rails, cement, square metres of housing, tons of wheat, metres of fabric, etc.), which were then proved insufficient to meet a diversified demand.

There are two ways to respond to such a challenge. One consists of giving market mechanisms their place, but that does not mean associating them with private property. It is therefore necessary to know how the markets involved in the general Plan are controlled and at the same time be concerned to reinforce the socialization of the management of the economy. This is indeed a highly delicate affair as the experience of the Chinese who chose this method bears witness because the drift towards the emergence of private capitalist forms is always present. The other way is based on the idea that a good centralized planning could forecast in detail in advance, using the most sophisticated means of modern information technology, an extremely diverse demand, even if, obviously, it means correcting the mistakes that are inevitable in all human activities. It is a question of a techno-mathematical ideal that is not altogether new (remember how the scholars in Saint Simon's government were imagining this) but, in my view it does not take into account how society really functions. Nevertheless the proof that this social imaginary still exists is provided by the proposals for 'perfect' (or nearly perfect!) socialist planning formulated, for example, by Cockshott and Cottrell. These proposals have won over certain visionaries of 21st century socialism (such as Jo Cottenier whom I shall discuss later).

The fact remains that after the death of Stalin, the rhetoric of so-called 'de-Stalinization' initiated by Khrushchev and the XXth Congress of the Communist Party in 1956 ignored this fundamental issue. Khrushchev's project was of a quite different kind: his aim was to denigrate the whole Stalinist period, to paint it in the blackest of terms, to ignore the challenges that the regime had had to face and not to recognize its successes. The convincing proof that Khrushchev lied (which is the title of a book by Gover Furr) is now available. At the same time Khrushchev undertook an absurd reform, which was to decentralize regionally this same Stalinist planning through the famous Sovnarkozes that only created utter chaos and much regression. This 'reform' was spiced up with a hollow discourse about a rapid catching up with the development of the more advanced countries. It was also associated with a so-called 'thaw' in the cold war, based on an ignorance of the real and permanent objectives of the imperialist powers that since 1917 have never renounced uprooting the hope of socialism.

Domenico Losurdo (in his book *Stalin*), Roger Keeran and Thomas Kenny (*Socialism Betrayed*) and Michael Lebowitz (*The Contradictions of "Real Socialism*) make it possible to correct the primary anti-Stalinist blunders à la mode, which are tirelessly repeated by the Western media and which have unfortunately been accepted by the heirs of eurocommunism.

The Soviet governing class put a swift end to Khrushchev's fantasies without, however, starting the indispensable reforms and choosing between the two paths described above. Thus the system was to retreat into the Brezhnevian Stagnation Period. Jo Cottenier (*L'économie du socialisme*) has made an in-depth study reviewing the reforms of the post-Stalin era, and I share his views so will present his main theme here.

The projects of Fedorenko, Nemchinov and Kantorowich, formulated in 1961 were based on mathematical and cybernetic methods and therefore they proceeded from the choice of a reinforced centralization but rendered effective through internal complexity. They were rejected by the Party and the State which inclined to favour more decentralization than centralization and thus preferred the reforms proposed by Liberman in 1962, based on strengthening enterprise autonomy and hence recourse to market mechanisms. Kosygin's reforms of 1965, which were inspired by Liberman, began the dismantling of planning and eventually were to authorize the belated liberalization of ownership relationships (which were implemented by Gorbachev on the advice of the openly pro-capitalist Aganbeyan).

During the long period of the Brezhnevian Stagnation Period nothing positive was undertaken. But much was in fact tolerated. The image of the 'Babushka dolls' (called matryoshka in russian) was used by Russian friends to explain the situation: inside a doll that represented a public enterprise was hidden a smaller doll representing a private one.

The Soviet system, which had been in decline for three decades, was incapable of undertaking effective reform and it ended with Gorbachev's perestroika. So the intentions of the last

PCUS Secretary General were unimportant as to whether he thought it possible to save the essentials of socialism in this way, or simply wanted to return to capitalism. He will go down in history as the architect of the disaster: the pure and simple restoration of capitalism and the break-up of the Soviet Union. It is understandable why he is considered as an absolute traitor by Russian public opinion. I myself heard Gorbachev speak at Rimini shortly after the collapse. I had the impression that he had never been a Marxist as he did not know the most elementary principles of Marxism. I concluded that he was just an apparatchik who could have made a career in any political system. The question then remains: how could such a person become Secretary General of a so-called Communist Party?

Basic characteristics of the late Soviet system

I define the late Soviet system by five basic characteristics: corporatism, autocratic power, social stabilisation, economic delinking from the global capitalist system and its integration into this system as a superpower. The concept of "totalitarian regime", popularised by the dominant ideological discourse is shown here as elsewhere to be flat and hollow, incapable of taking account of Soviet reality, its methods of management and the contradictions that led to the fall..

One: A corporatist regime

By corporatist regime I mean that the working class (supposed to become "ruling" class) had lost its unifying political consciousness both through the purpose of the policies put in place by those in power and through the objective conditions of the rapid mushrooming of their number during accelerated industrialisation. The workers of each enterprise, or group of enterprises forming a "combinat", together with their management and directors constituted a social/economic "block" and defended their place within the system. These "blocks" confronted each other on all levels: in negotiations (bargaining) between ministries and departments of Gosplan and in daily dealings with enterprises from combinats other than their own. The unions, reduced to work management (work and employment conditions) and the social benefits of the workers concerned, found their natural place in this corporatist system.

The corporatism in question had a crucial role to play in the reproduction and expansion of the system as a whole. It involved a double substitution: (i) of the principle of "profitability" that in the last resort governs decisions to invest in capitalism, and (ii) of the market that in capitalism still defines the way in which prices are determined. Corporatism constituted the reality that "planning" hid through its intentions to gain acceptance for a "so-called scientific rationale" of the macro-economic management of the production system.

Corporatism emphasized the regionalist dimension in the negotiations/bargaining between competing blocks. This regionalism was not based on the principle of "national" diversity (as in Tito's Federal Yugoslavia). The relationship between Russia—the dominant nation both numerically and historically – and other nations was not a "colonial" one. The redistribution of investment and social benefits that operated to the detriment of the "Russians" and to the benefit of the peripheral regions bear this out. In this regard, I do not accept the nonsense of comparing the USSR to an "imperial" system dominating its "internal colonies" in spite of the impression of the "dominance" of the Russian nation (and even the arrogance of some of its expressions). The regionalism in question concerned small regions (within the republics to which they belonged) with common interests to defend in a global system that ensured their independence which was in fact always more unequal than Gosplan's rationalising discourse claimed.

Two: Autocratic power

The choice of the term is not intended to weaken the critique of the system, "the absence of democracy" is easy to see whether representative (elections here bore no surprises) or participative proposed, naturally, as imagined by the revolutionaries of 1917, the unions and all possible forms of social organisations that had been submitted to central State control , thus effectively prohibiting participation in decision-making on all levels.

But this fact provides no explanation of the pseudo-concept of "totalitarianism". Autocratic power was disputed within the ruling class – the representatives of the corporate blocks. What to outward appearances was an autocracy masked the reality of a power that rested on the "peaceful" resolution of corporatist conflicts through consideration for one another.

Here again, the autocratic management of the conflicts in question necessarily took on regional dimensions. The structure of the system comprised a pyramid of powers that fitted together ranging from management (always autocratic) of local interests to those of the Union and the Republics. This regional dimension, sometimes but not necessarily "ethnic", facilitated the break-up of the Union and the threatened break-up of the Republics (Russia first) which is today a dangerous challenge for central powers.

Three: Stabilised social order

It is not my intention to ignore the extreme violence that accompanied the building of the Soviet system. These violent acts were of different kinds. The major conflict pitted the defenders of the socialist plan at the origin of the revolution against "realists" who, in practice if not in their rhetoric, gave absolute priority to "catching up" through accelerated industrialisation-modernisation. This conflict was the inevitable result of the objective contradiction that the revolution faced. It was necessary to "catch up", (or at least reduce the gap) as the revolution inherited a "backward" country (I find the expression "peripheral capitalism" preferable), and simultaneously build "something else" (socialism). I have stressed this contradiction, which I placed at the heart of the problems related with overcoming capitalism on a world scale (the "long transition from capitalism to global socialism"), and will not return to it here. The victims of this first major cause that led power to resort to violence were communist militants.

A second type of violence accompanied accelerated industrialisation. Some aspects of this type of violence can be compared to the type of violence that accompanied the construction of capitalism in the West, the massive migration from the countryside to the towns and the wretched circumstances associated with proletarianization (overcrowded accommodation, etc.). The fact remains that the USSR carried out this construction in record time – a few decades – compared with the entire century it took in central capitalist countries. The latter benefited from the extra advantages of their dominant imperialist positions and the option of allowing their "surplus" population to emigrate to the Americas. The violence of the primitive accumulation in the USSR is, in this respect, no more tragic than it was elsewhere. On the contrary, no doubt, for the accelerated industrialisation in the USSR allowed the children of the popular classes to benefit from massive social mobility unknown in the systems of the countries of central capitalism dominated by the bourgeoisie. In spite of everything else, it is this "specificity" inherited from original socialist intentions that won the majority of the working classes and even "collectivised" peasantry over to the system, even if autocratic.

It is not a question of excusing these violent acts, still less the criminal drifts that are associated with them and which could have been avoided. Nevertheless, it is important to compare them with the violent acts associated with capitalist accumulation. The latter have been responsible for the genocide of the American Indians, the slave trade, the colonial massacres (conquering soldiers celebrating by exhibiting the severed heads of those who resisted them). And this barbarism continues under our very eyes with NATO's military interventions whose objective is nothing less than to systematically destroy societies suspected of being able to resist them, as in Yugoslavia, Libya, Iraq and Syria. The victims of capitalist barbarism can be counted in hundreds of millions.

The Soviet system, however contradictory it may have been, succeeded in building a social order capable of stability which was in fact stable during its post-Stalin period. Social peace was "bought" by moderation in the exercise of power (although still autocratic), the improvement of material conditions and tolerance of "illegal" discrepancies.

Certainly, stability of this kind is not destined to last "eternally" but no system is, in spite of the claims made by ideological discourse (be it "socialist" or capitalist "liberalist"). Soviet stability masked the contradictions and limitations of the system which summed up its difficulty in passing from extensive forms of accumulation to intensive forms of the latter, like its difficulty in emerging from autocracy and allowing the democratisation of its political management. Yet this contradiction might have found a solution in an "evolution" towards what I described as the "centre left": the opening-up of market spaces (without challenging the dominant forms of collective property) and democratisation. Perhaps this was the intention of Gorbachev, whose failed attempt – naïve in many ways – brought down the regime "on the right" from 1990 onwards. Objectively the dismantling of the Soviet Union and the restoration of capitalism constitute what rightly the Russian people consider a treason.

Four: Economic delinking of the Soviet system

For the most part, the Soviet production system was effectively delinked from the dominant global capitalist system. I mean by this that the rationale that governed the economic decisions of those in power (investments and pricing) did not derive from demands for "open" integration into globalisation. It is thanks to this disconnection that the system succeeded in progressing as swiftly as it did.

This system was not, however, "wholly" independent of the

"rest of the (capitalist) world". No system can be and the delinking, in my definition of the concept, is not a synonym of "autarchy". Through its integration in the global system, the USSR occupied a "peripheral" position, mainly as an exporter of raw materials.

Five: Military and political superpower

Through the success rather than the failure of its construction, the USSR succeeded in working its way up to the rank of military superpower. It was the Soviet army that defeated the Nazis then, after the war, succeeded in record time in ending the United States' nuclear and ballistic monopoly. These successes are at the origin of its political presence on the post-war world scene. In addition, Soviet power benefited from the prestige of its victory over Nazism and that of "socialism", which it claimed to be the expression of, whatever the illusions concerning the reality of this "socialism" (sometimes described as "really existing socialism"). It made "moderate" use of it in this sense, contrary to the affirmations of anti-Soviet propaganda, it did not set out to "export the revolution" or to "conquer" western Europe (the spurious motive used by Washington and European bourgeoisies to get NATO accepted). It did, however, use its political (and military) might to compel dominant imperialism to pull back from the third world, opening up a margin of autonomy for the dominant classes (and the peoples) of Asia and Africa which they lost with the fall of the USSR. It is not by chance that the United States' hegemonic military offensive developed with the violence we have witnessed from 1990 onwards. Soviet presence from 1945 to 1990 imposed a "multi-polar" organisation on the world.

Thermidor, the Restoration: Toward a second wave of revolutionary advances?

The Russian and the Chinese revolutions had difficulty in

achieving stability because they were forced to reconcile support for a socialist outlook and concessions to capitalism. Which of these two tendencies would prevail? These revolutions only achieved stability after their "Thermidor," to use Trotsky's term. But when was the Thermidor in Russia? Was it in 1930, as Trotsky said? Or was it in the 1920s, with the NEP? Or was it the ice age of the Brezhnev period? And in China, did Mao choose Thermidor beginning in 1950? Or do we have to wait until Deng Xiaoping to speak of the Thermidor of 1980?

It is not by chance that reference is made to lessons of the French Revolution. The three great revolutions of modern times (the French, Russian, and Chinese) are great precisely because they looked forward beyond the immediate requirements of the moment. With the rise of the Mountain, led by Robespierre, in the National Convention, the French Revolution was consolidated as both popular and bourgeois and, just like the Russian and Chinese Revolutions, which strove to go all the way to communism even if it were not on the agenda due to the necessity of averting defeat, retained the prospect of going much further later. Thermidor is not the Restoration. The latter occurred in France, not with Napoleon, but only beginning in 1815. Still it should be remembered that the Restoration could not completely do away with the gigantic social transformation caused by the Revolution. In Russia, the restoration occurred even later in its revolutionary history, with Gorbachev and Yeltsin. It should be noted that this restoration remains fragile, as can be seen in the challenges Putin must still confront. In China, there has not been (or not yet!) a restoration.

The page of the 1917 Revolution has been turned and in general the first wave of revolutionary advances towards the emancipation of human beings and societies that it inspired has evaporated. Are the peoples forced to resign themselves definitively, renouncing the creative utopia of communism and remaining content to make their claims by adapting to eternal capitalism for ever?

And yet capitalism was not miraculously constituted all at once in the 16th century in the London/Amsterdam/Paris triangle, as the Eurocentric legend has it. Its incubation lasted ten centuries.

But, while the successive advances carried out in China as from the 10th century, in the Abbasid Caliphate and then the Italian cities did not lead to the crystallization of this new stage in the history of humanity, they nevertheless produced elements enabling this later crystallization in Atlantic Europe. Therefore, why should the invention of communism, conceived as a superior stage of civilization, not emerge through the unfurling of successive revolutionary advances?

References

Amin, S: *Ending the Crisis of Capitalism, or Ending Capitalism.* Fahamu Books , Oxford, 2010

Amin, S: 'China 2013'. *Monthly Review*, 64 (10) 2013

Amin, S: *Mémoires*. Paris: Les Indes Savantes, 2013

Amin, S: *Russia and the Long Transition From Capitalism to Socialism.* New York: Monthly Review Press, 2016, chapters 3,4,5,6

Amin, S: *The Implosion of Contemporary Capitalism.* London: Pluto Press, 2014

Bukharin, N: *Der Imperialismus und die Akkumulation des Kapitals.* Vienna/Berlin: Unter dem Banner des Marxismus, 1925-6, Vol II.

Cottenier, J: *L'Économie du Socialisme* (manuscript in French, in press in Belgium) ; the book mentions the works of Cockshott and Cottrell.

Furr, G: *Khrushchev Lied.* Kettering, Ohio: Erythros Press and Media, LLC, 2011

Furr, G: *Trotsky's Amalgams*. Erythros Press and Media, LLC, 2015

Gauthier, F: 'Albert Mathiez, historien de la Révolution Française', *Annales historiques de la Révolution française*, 353, juillet-septembre 2008 : Un siècle d'études révolutionnaires 1907-2007

Geoffrey R: *Stalin's Wars : From the World War to the Cold war 1939-1953*. Yale University Press: 2006. important preface of Annie Lacroix Riz in the French edition of the book.

Hobsbawm, E: *Echoes of the Marseillaise*. London:Verso, 1990

Kautsky, K. *The Agrarian Question*, Vol I. London: Zwan Publications. 1988(first German edition 1899)

Keeran, R and Kenny,T: *Socialism Betrayed: Behind the Collapse of the Soviet Union*. Indiana: Iuniverse Inc. 2010

Lebowitz M: *Contradictions of Real Socialism: The Conductor and the Conducted*. New York: Monthly Review Press, 2012

Lenin, VI: *Imperialism, the Highest Stage of Capitalism*. Penguin Classics, 2010 (first Russian edition 1917)

Marcuse, H: *One-Dimensional Man: Studies in the Ideology of Advanced Industrial Society*, 2nd Edition. Boston: Beacon Press 1991

Orwell, G: *1984*. London: Secker and Warburg, 1949

Revolution—A magazine published in Paris in 1963

Tinbergen, J: *Shaping the World Economy; Suggestions for an International Economic Policy*. New York: Twentieth Century Fund, 1962

3.

Reading Capital, reading historical capitalisms

– 1 –

Marx's major work—*Capital*—presents a rigorous scientific analysis of the capitalist mode of production and capitalist society and how they differ from earlier forms.

Volume 1 delves into the heart of the problem. It directly clarifies the meaning of the generalization of commodity exchanges between private property owners (and this characteristic is unique to the modern world of capitalism, even if commodity exchanges had existed earlier), specifically the emergence and dominance of value and abstract social labor. From that foundation, Marx leads us to understand how the proletarian's sale of his or her labor power to the "man with money" ensures the production of surplus value that the capitalist expropriates, and which, in turn, is the condition for the accumulation of capital. The dominance of value governs not only the reproduction of the economic system of capitalism; it governs every aspect of modern social and political life. The concept of alienation points to the ideological mechanism through which the overall unity of social reproduction is expressed.

Volume 2 demonstrates why and how capital accumulation functions, more specifically, why and how accumulation successfully integrates the exploitation of labor in its reproduction and overcomes the effects of the social contradiction that it represents. The suitable division of social labor between production of the means of production and production of consumption goods ensures the overall balance of supply and demand for goods and services produced exclusively within the context of the capitalist system of social relations. For my part, I have argued more specifically that: (i) the mechanism of accumulation requires an advance of credit the volume of which can be calculated on the basis of the rates of progress in the productivity of social labor for each of the two departments of production in question (and that was my response to Rosa Luxemburg's poorly-posed question concerning the realization of surplus value); (ii) the realization of a dynamic balance of growth requires that the real wage (the value of labor power) itself increase at a rate that can be calculated on the basis of growth in productivity; and (iii) consequently, the model presented in volume 2 does not allow us to say anything about the tendency of the rate of profit. (*LWV*, Chapter 1).

Taken together, volumes 1 and 2 of *Capital* do not provide us with specific information on the history of the emergence of the capitalism that they analyze. As Marx himself says: his aim is to offer an analysis of the essence of capitalism, its "ideal average." He does not consider, then, the relations between the space controlled by this capitalist mode (the only space analyzed in these two volumes) and other spaces of social production, prior to or even contemporary with the existence of concrete historical capitalism, in England or elsewhere.

This focus on the capitalist mode of production allows Marx to show us how that mode is the basis both for the emergence of an "economic science" that proposes to outline the conditions for the realization of a general equilibrium between supply and demand of capitalist commodities and for the subsequent assertion of that science as the newly dominant social thinking. Commodity alienation is the secret of this triumph. It reverses the relations between the economic instance, which becomes dominant, and the political and ideological instances, which consequently lose the characteristic dominance they had in earlier societies. This is the meaning of my reading of the subtitle of *Capital* ("Critique of

Political Economy"): a reading that reveals the status of economic science in modern social thought.

Volume 3 of Capital is different. Here Marx moves from the analysis of capitalism in its fundamental aspects (its "ideal average") to that of the historical reality of capitalism. He does so only partially by dealing with three sets of questions.

The first set concerns ground rent, that is, the right of landowners to a fraction of the surplus value produced by the capitalist exploitation of labor. We are here plunged into the heart of the question concerning the history of the emergence of historical capitalism. Capitalism did not fall from the sky onto a virgin earth. It was forged through its conflict with the feudal society of the Ancien Régime—in England, France, and a few other places in Europe. Traces of this conflict can be found in the capitalist formations (as distinct from the capitalist mode of production) that existed in Marx's era.

The second set concerns questions about the functioning of money (commodity money—the general equivalent of exchange—and credit, of which commodity money is the support). The distinction between interest on money (and its rate) and profit on capital emerges from this analysis. This is both an inseparable complement to the analysis of the capitalist mode of production (i.e., a complement to what volumes 1 and 2 contribute to this analysis) and an opening to historical considerations. In this connection, Marx offers several observations on the management of money by the Banks of England and France and on the theories advanced in this area by others.

The third set focuses on the cycles and crises of accumulation, examined within the context of the concrete history of England and Europe of that period.

Here I refer the reader to what I have written about Marx's analysis of these questions, both their general theoretical dimension and their concrete historical expressions (*LWV*, Chapters 2 and 3). Further, note that there is no systematic analysis in volume 3 of two sets of major questions: (i) the class struggles characteristic of the capitalist mode of production and of historical capitalisms, as well as the interaction of those struggles with the process of accumulation; and (ii) the new international relations distinctive of historical capitalisms, including capitalism's tendency towards globalization, and the interaction of these distinctive international relations with class struggles and the accumulation process. Marx provides only scattered observations on this subject.

– 2 –

To move from the reading of *Capital* (and particularly of volumes 1 and 2) to that of historical capitalisms at successive moments of their deployment has its own requirements, even beyond reading all of Marx and Engels. Marxist theoreticians and activists have always expressed their admiration for Marx and Engels's writings, made their reading of these writings recognizable, either explicitly or implicitly, and wanted to be inspired by them as part of their response to the challenges facing them in their struggles. I have no intention here of reviewing these diverse readings, but only to formulate what, in my reading of historical capitalisms, should be retained and discussed by all those—Marxist or not—who believe that "another, better world is necessary."

The reading of *Capital* that I have proposed above is certainly shared by others. But it is not the one prevalent in the dominant currents of the historical Marxisms of the Second and Third Internationals. The success of Marxism in revolutionary anticapitalist circles of the modern world necessarily involved a dose of simplification and popularization. Kautsky produced the first of what could be called a handbook of Marxism, something that Soviet Marxism popularized even more. In contrast with these abridgements, some Marxological works restore what, in my opinion, is the rightful status of *Capital*. It remains the case, though, that Marxology almost always favors exegesis to the detriment of a confrontation between theory and reality.

The recognition of this two-fold weakness—popularization and exegesis—should make it easier to understand the reasons behind the abandonment of Marxism characteristic of our era. *Capital* analyzes 19th century English capitalism and a reading of it does not allow us to understand the nature of contemporary capitalism. Marx's work is thus described as "outdated." That is not my opinion, not because I make Marx into an inspired prophet who is always right by definition and foresees everything, but simply because *Capital* allows us to grasp the essential foundations of capitalism beyond its historical forms and development. In this sense, reading *Capital* will continue to provide us with guidance to perceive the diversity of forms in which the history of capitalism is expressed, but nothing more. It is still necessary to interpret historical capitalism, something that is not found in *Capital*.

Will we find such an interpretation elsewhere in the other writings of Marx and Engels, perhaps partly in Volume 3 of *Capital*? I believe the answer to this question is no.

Certainly, Marx devoted many of his writings to analyses of the historical capitalisms of his era. He examined the complex political and social struggles that traversed them, without reducing them to the class struggle between the proletariat and bourgeoisie. He recognized the importance of the conflicts with the aristocracies of the Anciens Régimes of England and France, but also elsewhere in Europe (Germany, Russia, and others). He gave full meaning to peasant struggles and their position in the formation of historical capitalisms. He granted complete significance to the differences in the ways that political life was managed in the various nations and emphasized the nuances in their ideological expressions. He even recognized the conflicts between the emerging nations of capitalism and their colonial conquests.

In the same spirit, Marx tackled the origins and concrete historical emergence of capitalism in England, Western Europe, and the United States. Beyond that, he initiated the study of colonial capitalism in Eastern Europe and the Americas. It is precisely because he had understood better than anyone what defines the nature of capitalism (volumes 1 and 2 of *Capital*) that he was able to grasp the significance of changes in earlier societies, those that allowed the emergence of historical capitalism in some places and did not allow it in others.

Reading all of these penetrating writings is always refreshing and full of insights. But it is not sufficient for two reasons. First, because all of these propositions that can be defined as building blocks for the construction of a materialist reading of history remain—and will continue to remain—subject to successive critical readings in the light of advances in our knowledge of the past. Once again, Marx is not a prophet beyond all possible error. The second reason is even more important: historical capitalism has continually developed and been transformed, beyond Marx. The new is not written in Marx; it must be discovered.

I am certainly not the first, or the only, one to have adopted this approach to pursuing the work begun by Marx. The Social Democrats, Lenin, Mao, and many Marxist theoreticians (like Baran or Sweezy) have shared this approach. I will not mention here non-Marxist or even anti-Marxist theoreticians who also have been devoted to the objective of analyzing contemporary reality, whether or not they describe it as capitalist. Once again, I will not review these various interpretations of the contemporary world, but will only express my point of view on the question.

– 3 –

The preceding analysis should allow the reader to place my reading of historical capitalism in relation to Marx and historical Marxisms. I intend to outline my interpretation in what follows, emphasizing contemporary capitalism, its systemic crisis, and possible responses to that crisis.

1. I think it is helpful here to summarize briefly my interpretation of the emergence of historical capitalism (in Europe) (*CN*). I rejected the theory of the five stages of universal history (primitive communism, slavery, feudalism, capitalism, socialism) as well as the Asiatic mode of production, supported by various schools of historical Marxism. Having defined feudalism as an incomplete (peripheral) form from the family of tributary modes of production, I based my explanation of the early emergence of European capitalism, which then imposed itself on the world, on the concept of unequal development (the way is paved more easily for new advances in the peripheries of a system than in its centers). The most advanced (central) tributary systems also included the pre-requisites for the emergence of capitalism (contrary to the Euro-centric prejudice). The failure of the first waves of the movement in this direction (China, Near East, Italian cities) appeared to me to be the expression of a general rule in human history: the new does not emerge suddenly and miraculously; the way to the new is paved with difficulty through successive advances and retreats. The same thing is true about the necessary and possible surpassing of capitalism. I do not believe that my contention on unequal development can be found in Marx, who appears to be continually indecisive on the issue. My reading of the *Formen*[1] left me unsatisfied. My general view of historical materialism (note that I say "view" and not "theory") led me to clarify the meaning that I gave to "under-determination" and to propose, on this basis, an interpretation of modes of articulation between the instances of the particular reality of each historical formation. The meaning that I give to the cultural instance is obviously not the same as that attributed to it by currently fashionable culturalist theories. I define communism, understood as a superior stage of civilization and not as "civilized" capitalism or capitalism without capitalist profiteers, precisely as the dominance of the cultural instance. The titles of the chapters in *Spectres of Capitalism, A Critique of Current Intellectual Fashions* demonstrate my intentions. Here I can only refer the reader to these analyses (*SC*, Chapters 3, 4, 5).

2. The globalized expansion of capitalism has always been polarizing at each stage of its development, in the sense that it has continually constructed the opposition between dominant imperialist centers and dominated peripheries. Primitive accumulation is continual. The dominant social thinking, which acts as an apologist for capitalism, is forced to ignore this reality so that it can promise to the peoples of the peripheries an impossible "catching-up" in and by means of capitalism. The currently fashionable thinking today has fostered the strong resurgence of this fatal illusion. Imperialism, which the currents of contemporary post-modernism claim is in the process of disappearing, is supposedly only a parenthesis in history, one that undertakes the real and homogenizing globalization of the advanced capitalist model. The emergent countries are allegedly proof of that possibility. I have rejected this naive, apologetic view and analyzed the emergent forms as a new stage of polarization (*ICC*, Chapter 2). I do not believe that Marx was ever absolutely convinced that the power of capitalist expansion would necessarily end up by homogenizing the planet, even if he seems to have suggested that view in a few scattered observations. On other occasions, he did not hesitate to denounce the impasse constructed by colonialism, outlining the possibility of socialism's emergence from the peripheries of the globalized modern system, as shown by some of his writings on Russia.

3. The reality of the globalized and polarizing capitalist system forces us to take into consideration local social struggles as they are articulated with major international conflicts, both those between the imperialist centers and the peripheries struggling for their liberation and those among the dominant central powers. Marx had intended to deal with this question in the two volumes of *Capital* that, in the end, were not written. To formulate a critical economic theory of the world system is, in my opinion, inherently destined to failure. This is why I have argued that, at some point, Marx would have given up this project (*TEM, part I*) Certainly, the economic science of globalized capitalism that is offered to us is nothing more than an apology for imperialist practices. Yet another merely economic theory of the world system is just as impossible. Here we must place ourselves within the broader field of historical materialism. In this way, we can articulate classes, nations, and states in a whole that makes sense and allows us to understand how the modern world system functions through all its economic, political, and ideological dimensions. What I just said about the major conflict of our time (beginning in the 20th century) is equally valid for the conflicts between the dominant central nations in the 19th and 20th centuries. Since historical capitalism was formed on the basis of the emergence of central nations (Great Britain, France, Germany, the United States, and a few others), the conflict among these nations cannot be reduced to their competition in a market in the process of globalizing by economic means.

4. Marx also proposed to deal systematically with the class struggle in a volume of *Capital* that he did not write. His scattered writings on this major subject do not fill the void.

In volume 2 of *Capital*, Marx demonstrates that the process of accumulation in a society reduced to the capitalist mode of production requires an increase in wages parallel to the increase in the productivity of social labor. Otherwise, general equilibrium is impossible. There would be an excess in the production of capital goods and consumption goods in relation to insufficient demand. Capitalism carries within itself this fatal contradiction: the dominant position of the bourgeoisie and the competition between capitalist companies makes it impossible for wages to increase at the necessary rate. Capitalism cannot, then, ever overcome this permanent crisis. And yet it has succeeded in substituting for this insufficient demand its horizontal expansion into forms of production that preceded it (small agricultural and artisanal production, small landed property, small trade, etc.). External colonial conquest has produced analogous effects. Sweezy quite accurately observes that it is not the crises of capitalism that are the problem, but the moments of prosperity in which these crises are overcome. To understand why that is so, we must place ourselves beyond the economic analysis of the capitalist mode of production and in the broader field of historical materialism. The moments of prosperity are explained by wars, German and Italian unity, waves of major innovations (textile machines, railroads, electricity, the automobile and airplane, information technology). This is why I do not see capitalism as the end of history, but rather as a short parenthesis (*ECC*). For my part, I have attempted to place social struggles in this broader context, in particular the major class struggle between the proletariat and bourgeoisie, and have offered some systematic observations on the subject concerning the effects of this struggle on capital accumulation. (*LWV, chapters 1,4; TEM part I*)

5. The interpretation of contemporary capitalism that I propose begins with Baran and Sweezy's observations on the necessity for a third department to absorb the surplus produced by capitalism's fatal contradiction. I have already said that this was, for me, a decisive contribution that has enriched Marx's analyses of historical capitalism (*TEM part II)).*

I shall summarize my central contentions on the transformations of contemporary imperialist capitalism in the following two points:

- We have moved from monopoly capitalism as developed between 1890 and 1970 to a new stage characterized by a qualitatively higher level of centralization of control over capital. Consequently, all forms of production have been reduced to sub-contract status, thereby allowing the monopolies (which I call "generalized" for this reason) to appropriate an always increasing fraction of the surplus value in the form of monopoly rent (*ICC*, Chapter 1). This qualitative leap, which was effected in a relatively brief period of time between 1975 and 1990, is expressed by the power assumed by an oligarchy (several thousand individuals) that monopolizes all economic and political power. We thus move from historical forms of "concrete" capitalisms (the description that I propose to designate the operational system of a bourgeois class made up of numerous private property owners of segments of national capital) to what I will call "abstract capitalism." I refer here to my analysis in these terms of the transformation of the law of value and, with this development, the separation of the system of prices from that of values (*ICC, Chapter 1, and TEM part I*).

- This transformation has led to the decline in the old conflict among the imperialist powers and its replacement by a new collective imperialism of the triad (United States, Europe, Japan). The imperialist powers no longer have another way to continue their domination over the immense peripheries of the system (85% of the world's population), which have become zones of permanent unrest. The emergence of this collective imperialism in no way means that there has been the concomitant emergence of a "world bourgeoisie" (even at the level of the triad or of Europe) and a "world state" that would manage a globalized capitalism, as suggested by certain theories I have criticized (*Pambazuka*). State and bourgeoisie remain national: American, British, Japanese, German, etc. There is no necessary agreement between the requirements for the functioning of the economic base of the system and those for the political and ideological instances that carry out its management functions. There is no over-determination of the instances. It is, on the contrary, their under-determination that characterizes the development of social life. The concept of over-determination implies a linear and determinist view of history. Under-determination—which appears much closer to Marx's view—allows us to understand possible obstacles in the evolution of societies and the various alternative responses to those challenges. A good example of this contradiction is the current crisis of the European system, which is incapable of overcoming the reality of national governments, and the foreseeable implosion of the European Union (*ICC*, Chapter 3)

The changes that I have described here entail extremely important consequences for the forms of political management of all national systems.

In the centers (the triad), the monopoly of power exercised by the new oligarchies (which are not exclusively Russian, as Western propaganda would like us to believe!) has already emptied representative electoral democracy of any relatively positive meaning that it had acquired in the past. The alignment of social democracy, which has become social liberalism, with the positions of the classical right—in other words, the contamination of everything by the liberal virus—has already undermined the credibility of and delegitimized this democracy. This tragic evolution opens the way to the rebirth of fascism in societies that are increasingly in total disarray. The absolute power of the contemporary oligarchy is a new reality in the history of capitalism. Its dictatorship has in effect even abolished the very existence of both right and left political parties, condemned trade unions to powerlessness, and enslaved a media reduced to nothing more than a clergy dedicated to serving the oligarchy exclusively. Unfortunately, this dictatorship is quite effective, at least up to now. In these conditions, the grandiloquent discourse on the emergence of "civil society" is laughable. The civil society in question is tolerated—even encouraged—quite simply because it leaves people helpless and powerless (*ICC*, Chapter 1).

In the peripheries, in general, the government is hardly more than the tool of local servants of domination by the imperialist monopolies of the triad. This new subaltern oligarchy, which has replaced the earlier national historical blocs, does not have sufficient legitimacy on which to base its power and can resort only to the permanent exercise of violence. This general observation, however, does not accurately describe the situation in several emergent countries (China in particular) and in countries still resisting imperialist domination (Cuba, Vietnam, some Latin American countries). It is clear that collective imperialism does not tolerate any refusal to submit completely to the requirements of the form of globalization it has constructed. The ambition of any government that wants to assert itself on the world stage as a national capitalism (I am not talking about socialist projects that want to go beyond capitalism) and become an active participant in fashioning the world system encounters the firm determination of the triad to deny it this right, as we can see in the fierce hostility towards Russia. Another globalization, based on multipolarity, is simply unacceptable for the triad. Consequently, the powers of the triad are involved in a permanent war against the rest of the world because no nation can indefinitely tolerate the unconditional submission demanded.

The current system of liberal globalization is not viable. The extreme centralization of power to the exclusive benefit of the oligarchies is manifested in the endless increase in the unequal distribution of income and wealth functioning on a stagnant economic base in the historical centers and, of course, it is also manifested in the over-exploitation of labor in the dominated peripheries and the pillage of their natural resources. This contradiction is only overcome by the endless headlong rush into more financialization of economic life. One might think that such a system is irrational. In this vein, naive reformers (Stiglitz, Amartya Sen, and others) claim that it would just be necessary to control financialization to get out of the impasse. They quite simply forget that the oligarchy draws its privileges from this system, which might be absurd for everyone else, but is beneficial for it.

The current crisis, then, involves centralization of control over capital. It is thus a systemic crisis. In ordinary crises, characterized by a U-shaped curve, the same economic logic that produces the recession functions, in turn, to foster the recovery after a relatively short interval of a few years during which adjustments are made through the devalorization of capital and the liquidation of uncompetitive companies. On the other hand, in a systemic crisis, characterized by a L-shaped curve, the possible recovery would require major structural transformations. In the present context, this would be precisely decentralization of economic control both at the national level in the centers and at the level of the world system. Faced with the determined opposition of the oligarchy, an effective reform necessarily implies the formulation of a radical project, one that opens the way to a challenge to capitalism itself (*ICC*, Chapter 4). Since there is nothing to indicate that such a radicalization is on the agenda, the systemic crisis, which began in the 1970s, is far from having reached its end.

The modern world experienced its first systemic crisis beginning exactly one century before the second. Capital responded to that by a leap forward in the concentration of capital (the first monopolies at the end of the 19th century), the deepening of colonial globalization, and financialization managed by the City of that era, exactly as it has done to deal with the current systemic crisis, and with results just as unconvincing (*ECC*, Introduction). The "belle époque" (for capital!) of illusions (1900-1914) was quite short. The response that history gave to this first systemic crisis was: the First World War, the Russian Revolution, the 1929 crisis, Nazism, the Second World War, the Chinese Revolution, and the reconquest of independence by the people of Asia and Africa. Nothing less! These responses were thus spread out over a wide spectrum: socialist revolution, fascism, consistent reformism, and national independence. Why, then, would this second crisis we are now living through not call for responses just as varied: a second wave of socialist revolutions, but also a second wave of fascisms?

As always, it is impossible to give any definite response to the question of the future, which is always open. But we can—should even—attempt to outline possible responses by continually analyzing current social, political, and ideological struggles and their articulation with international conflicts, particularly with the major conflict between the collective imperialism of the triad and the rest of the world. We may begin by examining the gigantic transformations in the social composition of countries in the North, South, and East. Here I shall outline what I believe are the most essential points.

In the developed centers, it is said that the working class—reduced to that fraction concentrated in the large factories of the Fordist era—is in numerical and political decline. Yet at the same time, proletarian status—defined as the situation of a worker who has nothing to sell but his or her labor power—is becoming more widespread. Already more than 80% of workers are wage earners among which I think it is useful to distinguish those who produce surplus value (the great majority) from those who do not (a minority) or are even (a small minority) direct servants of the managers of capital (*TEM part III*). Independent workers are also sellers of labor power. Their independence is only an appearance because, in fact, they sell their services as sub-contractors to capital. But simultaneous with the rise in proletarianization is its extreme segmentation based on numerous criteria (women, youth, immigrant, precariously employed, unemployed, etc.) (*ICC*, Chapter 1). The immediate consequence of this segmentation, systematically implemented by current policies, is that the proletarianized population encounters great difficulties in its struggles to move from defending its gains to the formulation of radical reforms, which is complicated by their disinvolvement in discredited political parties. This situation results in the spread of illusions, the most serious of which encourage the rebirth of various kinds of fascism. But it also results in the naive idea advanced by postmodernist currents that civil society is capable of "changing life," while it is not even able to "change the government!" The center of gravity of struggles, then, is displaced towards fields of action viewed as critical for certain aspects of social life, particularly gender and ecological challenges. Let me be clear that I do not believe that these are minor problems, far from it. Marx already included in his critique the disequilibrium produced by the logic of capitalism in the metabolism between nature and human beings, a disequilibrium that has since become extremely dangerous. What many contemporary ecologists do not understand, unfortunately, is that re-establishing the equilibrium is impossible without a radical break with the logic of capital. Furthermore, it is unfortunately true historically that socialist movements have rarely acknowledged the central importance of relations between men and women. "First make the revolution, then deal with this problem." No, struggles on these two fronts are inseparable. No social advance is possible without a simultaneous advance in gender relations, at each stage of humanity's movement towards emancipation. No solid advance will be possible without an articulation of all struggles in a conscious, overall movement that would then be capable of attacking and destroying the fortress of generalized monopoly capitalism. Unfortunately, it is clear that the current struggles in the West are occurring without any interest in what is happening elsewhere in the world. Anti-imperialist solidarity has disappeared. Wars launched by the imperialist oligarchies are even supported and there is little awareness of the lie that hides the reality of the objectives of such wars. This is not the least of the successes of the dictatorship of the oligarchies and the use they make of their media clergy.

The changes that have affected the societies of the South and the formerly socialist East in recent decades have been equally large. Although these social transformations appear to be different from one country to another, they all follow the same logic, imposed by neo-liberal imperialist globalization. Consequently, these changes have been much more dramatic in their social, political, and economic effects than in the dominant centers.

The dominant major tendency has been to accelerate the processes that destroy the peasant societies that previously encompassed a large majority of the population in Asia and Africa. The peasant question immediately raises, with violent clarity, the related question of unequal relations between men and women because the destruction of rural societies always ends in more poverty and oppression of women. I have analyzed the forms taken by this accelerated and extremely brutal destruction elsewhere (*ECC*, Chapter 5). This destruction is not compensated by the necessary rate of increase in urban employment to alleviate the resulting human tragedy—and cannot be. Historical imperialist capitalism has nothing to offer other than the construction of a planet of slums. Obviously, desperate migratory pressures are also a consequence of this process of large-scale pauperization. In urban areas, pauperization is expressed in the very rapid growth of survival activities, which are described as informal employment. The systematic policies of planned exclusion that are implemented make possible the over-exploitation of subcontract labor to the benefit of monopoly capital.

Concomitant with these tragic developments that affect the vast majority of the people in these countries—60 to 80% of the population—the process of liberal globalization encourages the rapid growth of new middle classes composed of the minority that is integrated into the system of production. This minority—most often of negligible numbers 50 years ago—today sometimes encompasses around a fifth of the population in these countries. This minority is clearly aware that it is the sole beneficiary of the system. The indiscriminate praise lavished by pro-imperialist propaganda instruments (World Bank and others) on the rise of this new middle class quite simply ignores that its price is nothing less than the pauperization of the majority.

This specific form of proletarianization/pauperization creates a political situation that is difficult to manage. The dictatorship of local oligarchies subjected to the commands of the imperialist triad has, consequently, become the only way to manage this permanent crisis. The political personnel who had carried out responsibility for the national popular governments in the earlier stage—the era of Bandung and Nonalignment, between 1960-1980—often subsequently aligned themselves with the new globalization in the hope of remaining in power and of being tolerated by the masters of the triad, as we can see with the U-turn by Nasser's successors in Egypt, Hafez al-Assad in Syria, and Boumediene in Algeria, or the changes in the ANC in South Africa, in the Brazilian PT, and others. But the power of the local oligarchies, even when they are supported by the middle classes that benefit from the system, remain illegitimate in the eyes of the pauperized majority, as demonstrated by the explosion of unrest in the Arab world and elsewhere. Yet these movements have not yet succeeded in going beyond the stage of angry outbursts. The viscous character of the class structure produced by the model of lumpendevelopment in question certainly explains the structural weaknesses of the revolts. Thus the way is easily opened to the short-term triumph of backward-looking false alternatives, based on religion or ethnicity.

6. I have attempted to outline in the analyses above my interpretation of the two-fold character of the current systemic crisis: a crisis in the power of the oligarchy tied to an unviable economic model and a crisis of the majority of people who are victims, but incapable of formulating a coherent alternative. This two-fold character of the crisis eliminates for the foreseeable future the possibility of revolutionary advances that would open the way to the surpassing of obsolescent capitalism. I have presented some propositions concerning the first possible steps for a movement that wishes to go beyond capitalism (*ICC*, Chapter 4).

Some time ago, I was struck by the analogy between our situation and that of the fall of the Western Roman Empire. I gave an evocative title to the conclusion of my book *Class and Nation* (1979): "Revolution or Decadence?" This book dates back to the beginning of the still ongoing long systemic crisis (*CN*).

The Roman Empire established a system that centralized the draining and use of the tributary surplus that it drew from the exploitation of the peoples that made up the Empire, a surplus that surpassed the requirements for reproducing and advancing the productive forces of that time period: everything went to Rome and the Italian provinces. This over-centralized draining of surplus eliminated the possibilities for progress in the Empire's provinces (Rome's "peripheries"). To overcome this blocked progress, then, it was necessary to make the Empire explode, that is, for the provinces to "delink." Simultaneously, the partial redistribution of the surplus to the Roman plebians, corrupted by "bread and circuses," eliminated any revolutionary prospect at the center of the system. The Roman Empire thus collapsed into chaos. The feudal system, characterized precisely by the decentralization of the draining and use of the surplus, had the way paved for it only "by force of circumstances," with barbarian invasions and political chaos occurring for centuries. This is why we do not refer to a "feudal revolution," but to Roman decadence. It was nearly ten centuries before the new decentralized system gave rise to a renaissance of civilization in feudal clothes, based on progress disseminated across Europe.

The analogy appears quite striking to me. The contemporary system also suffers from an excessive centralization of the surplus, now drained in the forms of globalized capitalism. This over-centralization weakens the aspirations of people in the imperialist centers for a radical transformation of the system and simultaneously condemns people in the peripheries to a *lumpendevelopment* with no prospects. Meeting the challenge requires the peripheries to delink and substitute sovereign national projects for unending adjustment to the impasse entailed in the exigencies of imperialist globalization.

The analogy inspired me to work out two possible forms of transition from one system to a higher stage of civilization. The higher form, which could be called revolutionary, is produced when, faced with a mode of production that has exhausted its historical potential, the societies in question consciously and intentionally construct a possible and effective alternative. To varying degrees, the bourgeois revolutions and the first wave of socialist revolutions may be viewed in this way and thus merit their description as revolutions. But history obliges us to take the other form of transition into account, which occurs without the active and conscious intervention of social actors. The passage to European feudalism provides a good example. It is precisely the real historical existence of these two forms of possible social evolution that caused me to reject the determinist interpretation of some historical Marxist schools and emphasize the underdetermination of instances.

Certainly, feudal decentralization was not the "end of history" any more than is the one I am proposing today through a deconstruction of the current form of globalization. Feudal deconstruction was itself gradually surpassed by a reconstruction of a centralized surplus. This reconstruction occurred in two stages. In the first one, the absolute monarchies of the Ancien Régime imposed a new national centralization in close relation with the European mercantilist system, itself really a transition to complete historical capitalism. In the second stage, in the 19th and 20th centuries, the construction of capitalist/imperialist globalization completed the centralization, now operating on a world scale. In a similar way, we could imagine the long transition to communism, viewed as a higher stage of civilization, occurring in two steps: first, through the deconstruction of imperialist globalization followed by the reconstruction of a truly alternate globalization based on the fundamental principle of the solidarity of individuals and peoples in place of the principle of competition between capitals and nations. I will not venture any further in a vain attempt to describe a better future and specify what would be uniform on a world scale and what would fortunately not be so. The future is open and will be what people make it. I am satisfied with tackling issues related to what the immediate, necessary, and possible responses are to the challenge, in other words, strategies for the initial steps in a possible advance in the desired direction.

Unfortunately, there is no reason to exclude the alternative of "civilization's suicide." History is cluttered with the corpses of societies that were not able to overcome their contradictions, which then became fatal. Marx already made that observation, resolutely choosing a non-determinist view of history. A mismatch among the instances can become fatal. This is expressed through the continual renewal of alienations that are superimposed on one another. The commodity alienation characteristic of capitalism and the alienations from earlier history mutually reinforce one another. Clarity of awareness, that is, the capacity to understand the nature of the system's contradictions and issues and on that basis formulate a coherent alternative and effective strategies of action, seems to be absent from contemporary history. The lucid social actor has disappeared. This is what happened in the Roman Empire. The people of that time paid the price by sinking into barbarism for centuries. But while Europe of that time succeeded in surviving the disaster, would the same thing happen in our era when the established governments have incomparable means of destruction?

Perhaps between the two extreme situations outlined here (the highest possible revolutionary awareness or its total absence) there are other "intermediate" possibilities: partial awareness emerges from particular struggles, for example, from the struggles of peasants or women for the defense of human commons or the struggle for respect of popular sovereignty. The progress of the convergence of these particular types of awareness would make it possible to advance towards the formulation of new ways to surpass capitalism. But note: it is not a question of simply evading a forced optimism. Increased awareness will not happen through successive adaptations to the requirements of capitalist accumulation, but through awareness of the necessity of breaking with those requirements. The most enlightened segments of the movement should not isolate themselves by brandishing their disdain for others. Rather, they should involve themselves in all struggles in order to help the others to advance their understanding.

References

Samir Amin's works mentioned in the text.

CN: Class and Nation, Historically and in the Current Crisis. New York: Monthly Review Press, 1980.

ECC: Ending the Crisis of Capitalism or Ending Capitalism? Oxford: Pambazuka Press, 2010. (Introduction; Chapter 5: Peasant Agriculture and Modern Family Agriculture).

ICC: The Implosion of Contemporary Capitalism. New York: Monthly Review Press, 2013.

LWV: The Law of Worldwide Value. New York: Monthly Review Press, 2013.

SC : Spectres of Capitalism, A Critique of Current Intellectual Fashions ; Monthly Review Press 1988. (Chapter 3: Is Social History Marked by Over-Determination or Under-Determination; Chapter 4: Social Revolution and Cultural Revolution; Chapter 5: From the Dominance of Economics to the Dominance of Culture: The Withering Away of the Law of Value and the Transition to Communism.)

TEM : Three Essays on Marx's Value Theory; MR Press 2013 (I: Social Value and the Price-Income System; II : The Surplus in Monopoly Capitalism and the Imperialist Rent; III : Abstract Labor and the Wage-Scale)

Pambazuka News: 'Transnational capitalism or collective imperialism?' http://www.pambazuka.org/global-south/transnational-capitalism-or-collective-imperialism 2011.

'Contemporary Imperialism', *Monthly Review* 67 (3)(July-August 2015): 23-36.

Notes

1. *Translator's note:* This refers to that section of Marx's *Grundrisse* usually entitled "Forms Preceding Capitalist Production." The reader can find a translation in Karl Marx, *Economic Manuscripts of 1857-58, in Karl Marx and Frederick Engels, Collected Works* (New York: International Publishers, 1975-2004), 28: 399-439; also *Grundrisse: Foundations of the Critique of Political Economy*, trans. by Martin Nicolaus (New York: Vintage, 1973), 471-514.

4.

Revolutions and counter-revolutions from 1917 to 2017

The North-South conflict between centers and peripheries is a central factor throughout the entire history of capitalist development. Historical capitalism merges with the history of the world's conquest by Europeans and their descendants, who were victorious from 1492 to 1914. This success provided the foundation for its own legitimacy. With the presumption of superiority, the European system became synonymous with modernity and progress. Eurocentrism flourished in these circumstances and the peoples of the imperialist centers were persuaded of their "preferential" right to the world's wealth.

We have been witness to a fundamental transformation in this phase of history. The South has been slowly awakening, clearly apparent during the 20th century, from the revolutions undertaken in the name of socialism, first in the Russian semi-periphery, then in the peripheries of China, Vietnam, and Cuba, to the national liberation movements in Asia and Africa and the advances in Latin America. The liberation struggles of peoples in the South—increasingly victorious—have been and still are closely linked with the challenge to capitalism. This conjunction is inevitable. The capitalism/socialism and North/South conflicts are inseparable. No socialism is imaginable outside of universalism, which implies the equality of peoples. In the countries of the South, the majority of the people are victims of the system, whereas in the North, the majority are its beneficiaries. Both know it perfectly well, although often they are either resigned to it (in the South) or welcome it (in the North). It is not by accident, then, that radical transformation of the system is not on the agenda in the North whereas the South is still the "zone of storms," of continual revolts, some of which are potentially revolutionary. Consequently, actions by peoples from the South have been decisive in the transformation of the world. Taking note of this fact allows us to contextualize class struggles in the North properly: they have been focused on economic demands that generally do not call the imperialist world order into question. For their part, revolts in the South, when they are radicalized, come up against the challenges of underdevelopment. Their "socialisms," consequently, always include contradictions between initial intentions and the reality of what is possible. The possible, but difficult, conjunction between the struggles of peoples in the South with those of peoples in the North is the only way to overcome the limitations of both.

European Marxism of the Second International ignored this essential aspect of capitalist reality. It viewed capitalist expansion as homogenizing (whereas it is polarizing) and consequently attributed a positive historical function to colonialism. Lenin broke with this simplified interpretation of Marxism, which allowed him to lead a socialist revolution in a semi-periphery of that era—his "weak link." But Lenin thought that the revolution would rapidly spread from his country to the advanced European centers. That did not happen. Lenin had underestimated the devastating effects of imperialism in those societies. Mao went further in his conception and implemented a revolutionary strategy in a country even more peripheral than Russia.

The central reality of the imperialist character of historical capitalism implies an inescapable correlate: the long transition to socialism occurs through unequal advances, mainly originating in the peripheries of the world system. There is no "world revolution" on the agenda whose center of gravity would be found in the advanced centers. Lenin, Stalin, Mao, Ho Chi Minh, and Castro understood that and accepted the challenge of "constructing socialism in one country." Trotsky never understood that. The limits of what it was possible to achieve in these conditions, beginning with the heritage of the "backward" capitalism found in the peripheries, accounts for the later history of the 20th century's great revolutions, including their deviations and failures.

In the other countries of the peripheries, the first victorious struggles that transformed the world were the product of the great popular anti-imperialist movements. Nevertheless, the leaders of these movements had not properly assessed the necessity of combining the objectives of national liberation with a break from the logic of capitalism. Instead, these movements fostered the myth of "catching up" with the centers by capitalist means within globalized capitalism in the aim of building national capitalisms developed along the same lines as those found in the centers. Consequently, the changes that could have been achieved by what I have called "national popular" governments were in reality quite limited and their rapid exhaustion soon collapsed into chaos.

The challenge from the socialist revolutions lay behind the fascist direction taken by the counter-revolution in the imperialist centers. Fascism simultaneously sharpened inter-imperialist conflicts, particularly between Nazi Germany and Japan, on one side, and their major opponents—the United States and Great Britain—on the other. These circumstances account for the alliance of convenience between the USSR, the United States, and Great Britain during the Second World War. It is easy to understand, then, why this alliance was ended by the Western powers in 1945.

The exhaustion of the possibilities in the socialist and national populist transitions has not, by itself, opened the way to new advances, in the East, South, or West. The important political forces behind the original successes, and a fortiori the peoples involved, have not properly assessed the reasons behind the limitations inherent to the advances of the 20th century. This is why the current counter-revolution led by the historical imperialist powers (the United States, Europe, and Japan) has been able to exploit the resulting chaos. For the time being, this chaos instead encourages illusory responses adopted by projects of so-called "emergence" on the part of some countries in the South as well as the irrational, and consequently fascist, deviations of others (as shown by the examples of reactionary political Islam and reactionary political Hinduism). In the imperialist centers themselves, the capitulation of socialist and national populist projects has not encouraged any critical analysis of capitalism, but, on the contrary, reinforces illusions on the virtues of advanced capitalism. Here the victory of the counter-revolution and the retreat from earlier accomplishments (the Welfare State) encourage, in turn, the rebirth of neo-fascist responses.

I have analyzed the questions raised in this introduction elsewhere, a summary of which may be found in the suggested references. In this chapter, I will focus on analyzing the reasons behind the powerlessness of the working classes in the countries of the central imperialist triad (United States, Europe, and Japan). This analysis emphasizes the political cultures of the peoples involved. A political culture is the product of a long-term history, which is always, of course, specific to each country.

Perhaps the reader will consider my "judgments" a little too harsh. They are indeed. My observations of the South are no less so. Incidentally, political cultures are not transhistorical invariants. They change, sometimes for the worse, but just as often for the better. What is more, I believe that the construction of "convergence in diversity" within a socialist perspective requires such change.

The United States

The political culture of the United States is not the same as the one that took form in France beginning with the Enlightenment and, above all, the Revolution. The heritage of those two signal events has, to various extents, marked the history of a large part of the European continent. US political culture has quite different characteristics.

The particular form of Protestantism established in New England served to legitimize the new American society and its conquest of the continent in terms drawn from the Bible. The genocide of the Native Americans is a natural part of the new chosen people's divine mission. Subsequently, the United States extended to the entire world the project of realizing the work that "God" had ordered it to accomplish. The people of the United States live as the "chosen people." Of course, the American ideology is not the cause of the United States' imperialist expansion. The latter follows the logic of capital accumulation and serves the interests of capital (which are quite material). But this ideology is perfectly suited to this process. It confuses the issue. The "American Revolution" was only a war of independence without social import. In their revolt against the English monarchy, the American colonists in no way wanted to transform economic and social relations, but simply no longer wanted to share the profits from those relations with the ruling class of the mother country. Their main objective was above all westward expansion. Maintaining slavery was also, in this context, unquestioned. The important leaders of the American Revolution were almost all slave owners and their prejudices in this area were unshakeable.

Successive waves of immigration also played a role in reinforcing American ideology. The immigrants were certainly not responsible for the poverty and oppression that lay behind their departure for the United States. But their emigration led them to give up collective struggle to change the shared conditions of their classes or groups in their home countries and adopt the ideology of individual success in the host country. Adopting such an ideology delayed the acquisition of class consciousness. Once it began to mature, this developing consciousness had to face a new wave of immigrants, resulting in renewed failure to achieve the requisite political consciousness. Simultaneously, this immigration encouraged the "communitarianization" of American society. "Individual success" does not exclude inclusion in a community of origin, without which individual isolation might become insupportable. The reinforcement of this dimension of identity—which the American system reclaims and encourages—is done to the detriment of class consciousness and the forming of citizens. Communitarian ideologies cannot be a substitute for the absence of a socialist ideology in the working class. This is true even of the most radical of them, that of the black community.

The specific combination of factors in the historical formation of US society—dominant "Biblical" religious ideology and absence of a workers' party—has resulted in government by a de facto single party, the party of capital. The two segments that make up this single party share the same fundamental liberalism. Both focus their attention solely on the minority who "participate" in the truncated and powerless democratic life on offer. Each has its supporters in the middle classes, since the working classes seldom vote, and has adapted its language to them. Each encapsulates a conglomerate of segmentary capitalist interests (the "lobbies") and supporters from various "communities." American democracy is today the advanced model of what I call "low-intensity democracy." It operates on the basis of a complete separation between the management of political life, grounded on the practice of electoral democracy, and the management of economic life, governed by the laws of capital accumulation. Moreover, this separation is not questioned in any substantial way, but is, rather, part of what is called the general consensus. Yet that separation eliminates all of the creative potential found in political democracy. It emasculates the representative institutions (parliaments and others), which are made powerless in the face of the "market" whose dictates must be accepted. Marx thought that the construction of a "pure" capitalism in the United States, without any pre-capitalist antecedent, was an advantage for the socialist struggle. I think, on the contrary, that the devastating effects of this "pure" capitalism are the most serious obstacles imaginable.

The avowed objective of the US's new hegemonic strategy is not to tolerate the existence of any power capable of resisting Washington's commands. To accomplish that, it seeks to break up all countries considered to be "too large" and create the maximum number of rump states, easy prey for the establishment of American bases to ensure their "protection." Only one state has the right to be "large": the United States. The US's global strategy has five objectives:

1. Neutralize and subjugate the other partners in the triad (Europe and Japan) and minimize their ability to act outside of American control;

2. Establish NATO's military control of and "Latin Americanize" parts of the former Soviet world;

3. Assume sole control of the Middle East and Central Asia and their petroleum resources;

4. Break up China, secure the subordination of other large states (India, Brazil), and prevent the formation of regional blocs that would be able to negotiate the terms of globalization; and

5. Marginalize regions of the South that have no strategic interest. The hegemonic ambitions of the United States are ultimately based more on the outsized importance of its military power than on the "advantages" of its economic system. It can then pose as uncontested leader of the triad by making its military power and NATO, which it dominates, the "visible fist" in charge of imposing the new imperialist order on all possible recalcitrants.

Behind this facade there is still a people, of course, despite its evident political weaknesses. Nevertheless, my intuition is that the initiative for change will not come from there, even if it is not impossible that the American drive for hegemony will subsequently come to clash with others, which could begin the movement for a fundamental transformation.

Can Canada or Australia be something other than an external province of the United States? It is difficult to imagine another Canada, despite the political traditions of English Canada and Quebec's cultural specificity. The major political forces—polarized along the linguistic dimension of their resistance—do not envision a delinking of the Canadian economy from the economy of their large neighbor to the south.

Japan

Japan has a dominant capitalist economy and, simultaneously, a non-European cultural ancestry. The question is which of these two dimensions will gain the upper hand: solidarity with partners in the "triad" (United States and Europe) against the rest of the world or the desire for independence, supported by "Asianism"? Analyses—even wild imaginings—on this topic could fill an entire library.

A geopolitical analysis of the contemporary world leads me to conclude that Japan will continue to follow Washington, just like Germany, and for the same reasons. I note here the long-term significance of Washington's strategic choices following the Second World War. The United States had then chosen not to destroy its two enemies—the only ones to have threatened the inexorable growth of the United States towards world hegemony—but, rather, to assist their reconstruction and push them to become faithful allies. The obvious reason is that, at the time, there was a real "communist" threat. But even today, Beijing remains an enemy as can be seen in the conflict over islands in the South China Sea.

Are there any indications of a popular and national reaction? Certainly, the slowing down of the economic miracle and the ossification of the single ruling party have barely breached the facade of conformism. But behind this is hidden, perhaps, an inferiority complex towards China, which frequently reappears. Yet, a rapprochement with China, possibly motivated by a challenge to this conformism, does not seem likely. First, because Japan's dominant imperialist capital remains what it is. Second, because the Chinese and Koreans know it, even beyond their—justified—suspicion towards their former enemy.

Great Britain and France

Is there more of a chance for a change beginning in Europe than in the United States? Intuitively, I believe so. The first reason for this relative optimism is because the nations of Europe have a rich history as the incredible accumulation of its imposing medieval vestiges indicates. My interpretation of this history is certainly not the same as dominant Eurocentrism, whose myths I have rejected. The counter thesis I have developed is that the same contradictions characteristic of medieval society that were surpassed by the advent of modernity occur elsewhere. Yet I reject with equal determination the "anti-European" ranting of some Third World intellectuals who probably want to be convinced that their societies were more advanced than those of "backward" medieval Europe. That ignores the fact that the myth of the backward Middle Ages is itself a product of the later perspective of European modernity. In any case, having been the first to cross the threshold of modernity, Europe has since acquired advantages that I believe would be absurd to deny. Of course, Europe is diverse, despite a certain homogenization underway and a "European" discourse. England and France are the pioneers of modernity. This blunt assertion does not mean that modernity did not have earlier roots, particularly in Italian cities and later in the Netherlands.

England went through a very tumultuous period of its history during the period of the birth of new capitalist (mercantilist) relations. It was transformed from medieval "Merry England" into somber Puritan England, executed its king, and proclaimed a republic in the 17th century. Then everything was calm. It invented modern democracy, albeit with restrictions, in the 18th century and then in the 19th experienced an open-ended accumulation of capital during the Industrial Revolution without major upheavals. Certainly, this did not happen without class conflict, which culminated in the Chartist movement in the middle of the 19th century. But these conflicts were not politicized to the point of calling the entire system into question. France, on the other hand, crossed the same stages through an uninterrupted series of violent political conflicts. It is the French Revolution that invented the political and cultural dimensions of capitalism's contradictory modernity. The French working classes were not as clearly developed as in England, which had the only true proletarians of the time. Yet, their struggles were more politicized, beginning in 1793, and then in 1848, 1871, and much later in 1936. At the latter time, they were organized around socialist objectives, in the strong sense of the term. There was no 1968 in England. There have certainly been many explanations given for these different paths. Marx was quite aware of them and it is no accident that he devoted most of his attention to analyzing these two societies, offering a critique of the capitalist economy from England's experience and a critique of modern politics from France's experience.

Britain's past, perhaps, explains the present, the patience with which the British people endure the degradation of their society. Perhaps this passivity is explained by the way British national pride has been shifted to the United States. The latter is not, for the British, a foreign country like others. It remains a prodigal child. Since 1945, England has chosen to align itself unconditionally with Washington. The extraordinary world domination of the English language helps the English people live this decline without, perhaps, even feeling it to the fullest extent. The English relive their past glory by proxy through the United States.

Great Britain remains a key power for Europe's future. Although Brexit heralds the inevitable breakdown of the absurd European construction, the political currents that lie behind its victory in the referendum do not question either liberalism's reactionary social order or alignment with the United States. Moreover, in the system of globalized liberalism, the City, Wall Street's privileged partner, remains in a strong position and financial capital on the continent cannot do without its services. Nevertheless, history has no more reached its end in Great Britain than elsewhere. But my feeling is that this country will be able to rejoin the path of change only if and when it cuts the umbilical cord attaching it to the United States. At the moment, I do not see the least sign of that.

Germany

Germany and Japan are the two reliable lieutenants of the United States, forming the real triad—the G3—(United States, Germany, Japan rather than North America, Europe, Japan).

Neither Germany nor Italy nor Russia would have succeeded in reaching capitalist modernity without the paths pioneered by England and France. That statement should not be understood to mean that the peoples of these countries would have been, for some mysterious reason, incapable of inventing capitalist modernity, solely reserved to Anglo-French genius. Rather, the possibilities for a similar invention existed only in other areas of the world—China, India, or Japan, for example. But once a people entered into capitalist modernity, it shaped its own path, whether as a new center or a dominated periphery.

I interpret the history of Germany using that fundamental method. In this way, I understand German nationalism, pushed by Prussian ambitions, as a compensation for the mediocrity of the bourgeoisie, deplored by Marx. The result was an autocratic form of managing the new capitalism. Yet, despite its ethnicist tone, this nationalism (in contrast with the universalist ideologies found in England and, above all, in France, and later Russia) did not succeed in uniting all Germans (hence the eternal problem of the Austrian Anschluss, still unresolved today). This, then, became a factor that favored the criminal and demented excesses of Nazism. But there was also, after the disaster, a powerful motivation for constructing what some have called "Rhenish capitalism," supported by the United States. This is a capitalist form that deliberately chose democratization copied from the Anglo-French-American model. But it is without deep, local historical roots, even considering the brief existence of the Weimar Republic (the only democratic period of German history) and the ambiguities, to say the least, of socialism in the GDR. "Rhenish capitalism" is not a "good capitalism" in contrast with the Anglo-American extreme liberal model or the statism of "Jacobin" France. Each is different, but all are ill from the same illness, i.e., a capitalism that has reached a stage characterized by predominance of its destructive aspects. Moreover, the sun has now set on "Rhenish" and "statist" capitalisms. Globalized "Anglo-American" capitalism has imposed its model exclusively on all of Europe and Japan.

In the short term, Germany's position in globalization under American hegemony, just like Japan's, seems to be comfortable. Resumption of expansion to the East through a type of "Latino-Americanization" of East European countries can encourage the illusion that Berlin's choice is a lasting one. This choice is easily satisfied with low-intensity democracy and economic and social mediocrity, and is reinforced by support for the European Union and the Euro. If the political classes on the Christian Democrat and liberal right and the Social Democrat left continue in their stubborn pursuit of this dead end, we should not exclude the emergence of right wing, even fascist-type, populisms, though that does not mean they would necessarily be remakes of Nazism. The electoral successes of the National Front in France illustrate the reality of the general danger in Europe. In the longer term, Germany's difficulties will probably worsen, not improve. Germany's current economic assets are based on standard industrial production (mechanical, chemical) that modernize by increasingly incorporating software invented elsewhere. But like elsewhere, there is always the possibility that the German people will become aware of the necessity of initiating a real change off the beaten track. I believe that if France (which would then carry Germany along with it) and Russia were to take more initiative, another future for Europe would be possible. This choice could also lead to a resumption of positive movements for change in Mediterranean and Nordic Europe, which have failed up to now.

Southern Europe

Italy was momentarily thrust into the center of critical analysis and action during the "long 1968" of the 1970s. The power of the movement was sufficient to influence, in a certain way, the "center-left" state of that time, despite the self-confinement of the PCI. This happy phase of Italian history is over. Now we can only examine the weaknesses of the society that made it possible. The incompletely developed sense of national citizenship can, perhaps, be explained by the fact that the rulers of the Italian states were most often foreigners. The people generally saw in them only opponents to deceive as much as possible. This weakness was expressed in the emergence of a populism that fed on a rising fascism. In Italy, as in France, the struggle for liberation during World War 2 had been a quasi-civil war. Consequently, the fascists were forced to hide in the decades following 1945 without ever having really disappeared. The country's economy, despite the "miracle" that had given Italians a good standard of living up until the current crisis, remains fragile. But unreserved support for the European choice, which completely dominates the entire Italian political space, is, I believe, the main reason for the dead end in which the country finds itself.

The same unthinking support for the European project has strongly contributed to the failure of the popular movements that put an end to fascism in Spain, Portugal, and Greece to realize their radical potential.

This potential was limited in Spain where Francoism simply died from the quiet death of its leader while the transition had been well prepared by the same bourgeoisie that had formed the main support of Spanish fascism. The three components of the workers' and popular movement—socialist, communist, and anarchist—had been eradicated by a dictatorship that continued its bloody repression until the late 1970s, supported by the United States in exchange for anti-communism and the concession of bases to the US military. In 1980, Europe set as a condition for Spain's joining the European Community that it also join NATO, i.e., that it accede to the complete formalization of its submission to Washington's hegemony! The workers' movement attempted to play a role in the transition through its "workers' committees" formed underground in the 1970s. It was unfortunately obvious that, not having succeeded in gaining the support of other segments of the popular and intellectual classes, this radical wing of the movement could not prevent the reactionary bourgeoisie from controlling the transition.

The revolt of the armed forces in Portugal that ended Salazarism in April 1974 was followed by a huge popular explosion the backbone of which was formed by communists, both from the official communist party and from Maoist currents. The defeat of this tendency within the ruling group eliminated the communist leadership to the advantage of all-too-timid socialists. Since then, the political sphere has settled back into sleep.

In Greece also, the choice in favor of Europe was not obvious following the fall of the colonels. During the Second World War, the communist party had succeeded, just as in Yugoslavia, in forming a single anti-fascist front. Greece and Yugoslavia not only "resisted" the German invaders, like others did; they continually fought a real war that played a decisive role in the instantaneous collapse of the Italian armies in 1943, thereby forcing the Germans to station a large number of troops on their territories. The Greek resistance, which became a revolution in 1945, was defeated by the joint intervention of the United States and Great Britain. The Greek right is, moreover, responsible for integrating their country into NATO, within which the European project takes shape, all to the exclusive benefit of the "cosmopolitan" comprador bourgeoisie.

The deepening of the systemic crisis of monopoly capitalism has led to an unparalleled social disaster in the fragile countries of southern Europe. It also strikes hard at the countries of Eastern Europe, reduced to little more than the semi-colonies of Western Europe, particularly Germany. It is easy to understand, then, the recent emergence of immense popular movements (Syriza in Greece, Podemos in Spain) that have won some exciting victories in their rejection of the extreme austerity policies imposed by Berlin and Brussels. Nevertheless, we must acknowledge that the general opinion in these countries does not yet envision the necessity of deconstructing the European system; most people prefer to bury their heads in the sand and convince themselves that this Europe is reformable. Consequently, their movements continue to be paralyzed.

Northern Europe

For different reasons, the Nordic countries have maintained, up to now, a suspicious attitude with regard to the European project.

Under the leadership of Olof Palme, Sweden attempted to follow a globalist, internationalist, and neutralist path. Beginning with the country's more recent European choice and the rightward drift of its social-democratic forces, the reversal has been quite abrupt. This reversal, however, forces us to look more closely at the weak points of Sweden's exceptional experience: Palme's perhaps too personal role, the illusions of the youth who, long confined to this relatively isolated country, belatedly discovered the world with a good dose of naivety after 1968, but also its somewhat tarnished, and long hidden, past during the Second World War.

Norwegian society was formed from small peasants and fishers, without the presence of an aristocratic class similar to that of Sweden or Denmark. Thus it is very much alive to questions of equality. This undoubtedly explains the relative power of its extreme left party and the radical proclivities of social democratic forces that, up to now, have resisted the siren's song of Europe. The Greens appeared in this country before organizing in the others. On the other hand, the country's membership in NATO and the financial affluence from North Sea oil (an affluence that is somewhat corrupting in the long term) certainly counteract these positive tendencies.

The independence that Finland gained without a struggle during the Russian Revolution (Lenin had already unhesitatingly accepted it) was less the product of a unanimous demand than is often admitted. The Grand Duchy already benefited from a large degree of autonomy in the Russian Empire, which was considered quite satisfactory by opinion at the time. Its ruling classes served the Tsar with as much sincerity as those of the Baltic countries. The working classes were not oblivious to the program of the Russian Revolution. That is why independence did not settle the country's problems, which were dealt with only at the end of the civil war, in the end barely won by the reactionary forces (with the support of imperial Germany and later the Allies). These forces later drifted towards fascism and became allies of the fascist powers during the Second World War. What is called "Finlandization," which NATO propaganda presented as unacceptable, was in fact only a neutralism (certainly imposed originally by the peace treaty) that could have formed one of the bases for a better European reconstruction than that of the Atlanticist alliance. Will European pressures, which have triumphed in the monetary area (with Finland's participation in the Euro), succeed in eating away at this interesting historical heritage?

Can one expect anything from Denmark with an economy that is too dependent on Germany's? This dependence is experienced neurotically, as can be seen in the ambiguous and confused series of votes on the question of the Euro. Yet I do not think that all-too-typical social democratic forces can offer a challenge to the current course. "The red-green alliance" is, consequently, rather isolated.

It is well known that the Netherlands was the site of the original bourgeois revolution in the 17th century, before England and France. But the modest size of the United Provinces prevented this country from achieving what its competitor students were able to do. Although the cultural heritage of this history is not lost, today the economic and financial system of the Netherlands functions within the mark/Euro environment.

Is Europe capable of moving out of its political insignificance in the modern world?

In the 1970s and 1980s, I thought that the formation of a north-south "neutralist" axis in Europe, made up of Sweden, Finland, Austria, Yugoslavia, and Greece, was possible, with positive effects on the countries of both Western and Eastern Europe. It could have encouraged the former to re-think their Atlanticist alignment and might have found a favorable echo in France. Unfortunately, De Gaulle was no longer there and the Gaullists had completely forgotten the general's reservations about NATO. Such an axis might have opened up possibilities for East European countries to move towards center left positions and thereby avoid their later fall to the right. This project might have initiated the construction of an authentic "other Europe," truly social and thus open to the formulation of a socialism for the 21st century that respected its national components, was independent from the United States, and facilitated a reform worthy of the name in Soviet bloc countries. This construction was possible, concomitant with the Europe of Brussels, at that time consisting only of a still limited economic community. I was even able to present these ideas to the leadership of the left in the countries concerned and had the impression that the idea did not displease them. But there was no follow-up.

The European lefts have not properly assessed the stakes and have supported the development of the European project led by Brussels. This has been a reactionary project from the beginning, devised by Monnet (whose fiercely anti-democratic opinions are well known, as shown in J.P. Chevènement's book *La Faute de Monsieur Monnet[i]*). The European project, along with the Marshall Plan devised by Washington, was designed to rehabilitate rightist forces (under the cover of "Christian democracy) or even fascists, reduced to silence by the Second World War, so as to nullify any scope for the practice of political democracy. The communist parties understood that. But at the time, the alternative of a "Soviet" Europe was already no longer credible. Their later unconditional adherence to the project was no better, even though it was disguised as "Eurocommunism."

Today, not only has the European Union trapped the peoples of the continent in an impasse, consolidated by the "liberal" and Atlanticist (NATO) choice, but has even become the instrument for the "Americanization" of Europe, substituting the US's culture of "consensus" for the European tradition's political culture of conflict. The ultimate adherence of Europe to Atlanticism is not unthinkable, based on awareness of the advantages from exploiting the planet for the benefit of the triad's collective imperialism. The "conflict" with the United States turns around sharing the booty, hardly more. If ever the project were carried out against everyone, then the European institutions would become the main obstacle to the progress of Europe's peoples.

European reconstruction, then, requires the deconstruction of the current project. Is it even thinkable today to question the European-Atlanticist project such as it is and construct an alternative Europe that would be both social and non-imperialist with regard to the rest of the world? I think so and even think that the beginning of an alternative project originating from anywhere would find favorable echoes throughout Europe in a short period of time. An authentic left, in any case, should not think otherwise. If it dares to do so, then I am one of those who believe that the European peoples can demonstrate that they still have an important role to play in shaping a future world. Short of that, the strongest probability is the collapse of the European project into chaos, which would not displease Washington. Europe will be socialist, if the left forces dare to make it so, or it simply will not be.

I believe that the change can only begin if France were to take some courageous initiatives in the right direction. That would then lead Germany to move in the same direction and, consequently, the rest of Europe. The way would then be open for a rapprochement with China and Russia. Europe's status on the international political scene is condemned to insignificance by its support for Washington's project for world domination. If it were to follow the path outlined above, it could then exploit its economic power for the reconstruction of an authentic multipolar world. Failing that, the "West" will remain American, Europe will remain German, the North-South conflict will continue to be central, and any possible advances will largely be confined to the peripheries of the global system; in other words, a "remake" of the 20th century.

§

In conclusion, I will again point out that the system of neo-liberal globalization has entered into its last phase; its implosion is clearly visible, as indicated by, among other things, Brexit, Trump's election, and the rise of various forms of fascism. The rather inglorious end of this system opens up a potentially revolutionary situation in all parts of the world. But this potential will become reality only if radical left forces know how to seize the opportunities offered and design and implement bold offensive strategies based on the reconstruction of the internationalism of workers and peoples in the face of the cosmopolitanism of the imperialist powers' financial capital. If that does not happen, then the left forces of the West, East, and South will also share responsibility for the ensuing disaster.

Supplementary readings

This chapter focuses on the societies of the imperialist triad. It is part of a larger set of recent analyses that I have advanced in the following works:

USSR and Russia

Amin, S: *Russia and the Long Transition from Capitalism to Socialism.* New York: Monthly Review Press, 2016 (particularly chapters 3-6).

Amin, S: 'The October Revolution Started off the Transformation of the World.' *International Critical Thought,* vol 7 (2), 2017

China

Amin, S: 'China 2013.' *Monthly Review* 64 (10) (March 2013): 14-33.

The larger South

Amin, S: "The Sovereign Popular Project: The Alternative to Liberal Globalization." *Labor and Society*, 20, (1) 2017

The ongoing implosion

Amin, S: *The Implosion of Contemporary Capitalism.* London: Pluto, 2014 (particularly chapters 2, 5).
Amin, S: 'Brexit and the EU Implosion: National Sovereignty—For What Purpose? *MR Online*, 2016. https://mronline.org/2016/08/08/amin080816-html/
Amin, S: 'The Election of Donald Trump.' *MR Online*, November 30, 2016. https://mronline.org/2016/11/30/amin301116-html/

The internationalism of peoples

Amin, S: *The World We Wish To See*. New York: Monthly Review Press, 2008 (particularly chapters 1-3).
Chevènement, J-P: *La Faute de Monsieur Monnet: La République et l'Europe.* Paris: Fayard, 2006.

5.

The sovereign popular project: The alternative to liberal globalization

Global capitalism as practiced today is actually a complex construction of states (sovereign nations in principle), peoples and nations (be they "homogenous" or not), and social classes based on the capital/labour conflict which is the bedrock of true capitalism. As such, conflicts between states and class struggles are interwoven in a close relationship of interdependence. The interdependence of social struggles in various countries of the world therefore depends on how the various dominant blocs exploit the possibilities at their disposal on the international scene. This on its part will depend on the value of their political and social projects. The establishment of global alliances of dominated classes which will create a "better global alternative" is therefore confronted with serious obstacles worth analysing.

The support or the rejection of national sovereignty gives rise to severe misunderstandings as long as the class content of the strategy in the frame of which it operates is not identified. The dominant social bloc in capitalist societies always conceives national sovereignty as an instrument to promote its class interests, i.e. the capitalist exploitation of home labour and simultaneously the consolidation of its position in the global system. Today, in the context of the globalized liberal system dominated by the financialized monopolies of the Triad (USA, Europe, Japan) national sovereignty is the instrument which permits ruling classes to maintain their competitive positions within the system. The government of the USA offers the clearest example of that constant practice: sovereignty is conceived as the exclusive preserve of US monopoly capital and to that effect the US national law is given priority above international law. That was also the practice of the European imperialist powers in the past and it continues to be the practice of the major European states within the European Union (I have discussed this question specific to Europe in *"The implosion of contemporary capitalism"*, chapter 4).

Keeping that in mind, one understands why the national discourse in praise of the virtues of sovereignty hiding the class interests in the service of which it operates has always been unacceptable for all those who defend the labouring classes.

Yet we should not reduce the defence of sovereignty to that modality of bourgeois nationalism. The defence of sovereignty is no less decisive for the protection of the popular alternative on the long road to socialism. It even constitutes an inescapable condition for advances in that direction. The reason is that the global order (as well as its sub-global European order) will never be transformed from above through collective decisions of the ruling classes. Progress in that respect is always the result of the unequal advance of struggles from one country to another. The transformation of the global system (or the subsystem of the European Union) is the product of those changes operating within the frame of the various states which, in their turn, modifies the international balances of forces between them. The nation state remains the only frame for the deployment of the decisive struggles which ultimately transform the world.

The peoples of the peripheries of that system, polarising by nature, have a long experience of that positive progressive nationalism which is anti-imperialist, rejects the global order imposed by the centres, and therefore is potentially anti-capitalist. I say only potentially because this nationalism may also inspire the illusion of a possible building of a national capitalist order able to catch up with the national capitalisms ruling the centres. Nationalism in the peripheries is progressive only at that condition, as long as it remains anti-imperialist, i.e. today conflicting with the global liberal order. Any other nationalism (which in this case is only a façade) which accepts the global liberal order is the instrument of local ruling classes aiming at participating in the exploitation of their peoples and eventually of other weaker partners, operating therefore as sub-imperialist powers.

The confusion between these two antonymic concepts of national sovereignty and therefore the rejection of any nationalism annihilates the possibility of moving out of the global liberal order. Unfortunately, the left—in Europe and elsewhere—does often make such a confusion.

Global really existing capitalism is imperialist in nature

The diversity of the social and political conditions in the states which make up the global system stems from the types of developments which define the global expansion of capitalism, subjected to the demands of accumulation in the centre of the system. Moreover, the history of the making of each country, whether dominant or dominated, has always been characterised by features which are unique to it. As such, hegemonic blocs of classes and interests that have enabled capitalism to assert its domination and those which victims of the system have established or tried to establish in order to face the challenges, have always been different from one country to another and from one period to another. These evolutions have shaped specific political cultures, setting up in their own ways value systems and "traditions" of specific forms of political expression, organisation and struggle. These diversities are very objective just like the cultures through which they are portrayed. Finally, the development of production forces in itself, through scientific and technological revolutions that define the contents, has on its part dictated changes in the organisation of work and various forms of its subjection to the demands of capitalist exploitation. All these different realities prohibit the reduction of political actors to the bourgeoisie/proletariat conflict.

Capitalism is based on a market integrated in its three dimensions (commodities market, financial markets, and the labour market). But really existing capitalism as a global system is based solely on the global expansion of the market in its first two dimensions, as the establishment of a real global labour market is hindered by the persistence of political state barriers, at the detriment of economic globalization which is as such always limited. For this reason, really existing capitalism is necessarily polarizing at the global level and the uneven development it creates is the most violent and growing contradiction of modern times that cannot be overcome within the framework of the logic of capitalism.

Development and "underdevelopment" are the two faces of the same reality: global capitalism. There is no scientific basis to the dominant discourse that links capitalism to the affluence of the countries of the centre and qualifies others (developing countries) as "retarded". Consequently, national liberation struggles of the people in the peripheries have always, objectively, been in conflict with the logic of capitalism. They are "anti-systemic" (anti-capitalist), though at varying degrees of the conscience of the actors and the radicalism of their projects. This situation calls for a long lasting transition to global socialism. If capitalism has set the foundation of an economy and a global society, it is however unable to carry on the logic of globalization to the end. Socialism, conceived as a qualitatively higher level of humanity, can for this reason be considered universal. However, its construction will have to go through a very long historical transition by using a strategy of the contradictory negation of capitalist globalization.

In its manifestation as a political and social strategy, this general principle signifies that the long transition calls for the indispensable establishment of a popular national society associated to an auto-centered national economy. Such a creation is contradictory in every aspect: it associates capitalist criteria, institutions and operational modes to social aspirations and reforms which are in conflict with the logic of global capitalism; it also associates an external exposure (controlled as much as possible) to the protection of the demands of progressive social transformation which conflict with dominant capitalist interests.

Due to their historical nature, governing classes generally formulate their visions and aspirations within the perspective of really existing capitalism and, willingly or unwillingly, subject their strategies to constraints of global capitalist expansion. This is the reason why they cannot really envisage a delinking. On the contrary, popular classes must give in to this whenever they try to use political power to transform their conditions and liberate themselves from the inhuman consequences which the polarizing expansion of capitalism subjects them to. The appraisal of the strategic choices of government policies and movements of the dominated masses in the global South should follow these criteria.

An inward-looking development option is indispensable

Historically, an inward-looking development ("self-reliance") has been a specific feature of the capital accumulation process in core capitalist countries and has conditioned the modalities of the resulting economic development, which is mainly controlled by the dynamics of internal social relations and strengthened by the external relations at their service. On the other hand, in the peripheries, the capital accumulation process is mainly derived from the evolution of countries of the centre in a way that consolidates "dependence".

The dynamics of the inward-looking development model is based on a major articulation: one which puts side by side the close interdependence of the growth of the production of goods for production and that of the production of goods for mass consumption. This articulation falls in line with a social relationship whose main terms are set up by the two main blocs of the system: the national bourgeoisie and the labour force. Inward-looking economies are not water tight entities in themselves; on the contrary, they are aggressively open in this direction such that they shape the global system in its totality through their potential political and economic intervention on the international scene. However, the dynamics of peripheral capitalism—the antinomy of central inward-looking capitalism by definition—is based on another main articulation that puts side by side the capacity to export on the one hand and consumption of a minority—imported or locally produced- on the other hand. This model defines the comprador as opposed to national—nature of bourgeoisies in the peripheries.

This contrast results in a divergent trend towards the integration of nations in the centres where centripetal forces dominate the inward-looking accumulation on the one hand, and on the other hand, towards the permanent disintegration threat of those of the peripheries due to the effects of centrifugal forces of dependent accumulation. Imperialist policies encourage such trends, defending them with arrogance and cynicism, with the excuse of the "right to interference", "humanitarian" interventions, and abusive rights "to self-determination".

The Awakening of the South

The deployment of imperialism was manifested from 1492 (not the date of the "discovery" of America, but the date of its conquest and the destruction of its people), and in the four centuries that followed, by the conquest of the world by Europeans. The people of Asia and Africa, American Indians who survived the genocide, and later on, the new nations of Latin America and the Caribbean, had to try and adjust to the demands of this subjection.

Such deployment of global capitalism/imperialism was for the affected people, the greatest tragedy in human history, thus demonstrating the destructive nature of the accumulation of wealth. For this reason, capitalism can only be a moment in history, with its continuous development leading to barbarism. It is an unsustainable system in the long term (and not the "end of history"!), not only for ecological reasons—though reasonable—but above all, for the devastating effects of mercantilism on individuals and whole peoples rendered "useless". The catastrophe manifested itself through the destruction of complete populations and the reduction of the proportion of non-European populations from 82% of the world population in 1500, to 63% in 1900.

Simultaneously, the misfortune of some was the delight of others. Accumulation through dispossession of total populations did not only lead to the wealth of the dominant classes of the Old Order, but above all, to the administrative and military reinforcement of European countries. The industrial revolution of the end of the XVIII century could not have been without this first period of imperialist deployment. On its part, the military supremacy of Modern Europe made the XIX century the peak of capitalism. The North-South gap widened and the apparent wealth ratio moved from 1 to 1.3 in 1800 (a ratio not always favourable to Europeans) to 1 to 40 today. The pauperization law formulated by Marx was more evident in the system than could be imagined by the father of scientific socialism!

This page in history is now closed. The people of the peripheries no longer accept the fate reserved for them by capitalism. This crucial change in attitude is irreversible and signifies that capitalism has reached its period of decline. A decline initiated by the 1917 Revolution, followed by the socialist revolutions of China, Vietnam and Cuba and by the radicalisation of national liberation movements in the rest of Asia and Africa.

The concomitance of these two forms of transformation is not by chance. This does not exclude the persistence of various illusions: that of reforms capable of giving a human face to capitalism (something it has never been able to do for the majority of people), that of a possible "catching up" within the system, which is the dream of the ruling classes of the "emerging" nations, exhilarated by the success of the moment; and that of backward-looking traditionalism (pseudo-religious or pseudo-ethnic) into which a vast majority of the "excluded" people of today have fallen. Such illusions seem to persist due to the fact that we are passing through a conjunctural low point. The wave of revolutions of the XX century is over, that of the modern radicalism of the XXI century is still to come. And like Gramsci wrote, there are monsters in the twilight of transitions. The awakening of the people of the peripheries was manifested from the XX century not only by their demographic growth, but also by their expressed intentions to reconstruct their country and society, wrecked by the imperialism of the four preceding centuries.

Bandung and the first globalisation of struggles (1955-1980)

In 1955 in Bandung, governments and people of Asia and Africa expressed their intention to reconstruct the global system on the basis of the acknowledgment of the rights of countries previously under domination. Such "rights to development" formed the basis of the globalisation of the period, which was implemented within a negotiated multi-polar framework and consequently imposed on imperialism, itself forced to adjust to these new realities.

The industrialisation process initiated during the Bandung period was not the result of the logic of imperialist deployment, but was imposed by the victories of people of the South. Such progress undoubtedly nurtured a "catching up" illusion that seemed to be underway, whereas imperialism, forced to adjust to the realities of the development of the peripheries, was recomposing itself around new forms of domination. The old contrast of imperialist countries/ dominated nations synonymous with the contrast of industrialized/unindustrialized countries, gradually gave way to a new form of contrast based on the centralisation of advantages associated with the "five new monopolies of imperialist countries" (the control of modern technologies, natural resources, the global financial system, means of communication and weapons of mass destruction).

The Bandung period was also that of African Renaissance. Pan-Africanism should be situated within this perspective. It is not by chance that African countries are involved in renovation projects with inspiration from the values of socialism, for the liberation of the people of the peripheries is actually anti-capitalist.

There is no need to denigrate these numerous attempts on the continent, as is the case today: in thirty years, the horrible regime of Mobutu led to the production of an education capital in Congo 40 times higher than what the Belgians achieved in 80 years. Whether we like it or not, African countries are at the origin of the creation of veritable nations. And the options (trans-ethnic) of the ruling classes favoured such crystallization. Ethnic deviations came later, caused by the erosion of the Bandung models, leading to the loss of legitimacy of powers and the recourse to ethnicity by some of those in power to reconstitute power for their interests.

New era, new challenges?

The dichotomy centres/peripheries is no longer synonymous with industrialised/unindustrialised countries. The polarization centres/peripheries which marks the imperialist character of the expansion of global capitalism is still underway, and is even gaining more ground through the help of the "five new monopolies" imperialist countries benefit from (mentioned above). In such conditions, the continuation of accelerated development projects in emerging peripheries, which has been an undisputable success (in China in particular, but also in other countries of the South), does not abolish imperialist domination. This deployment instead sets up a new centres/peripheries contrast rather than eroding it.

Imperialism cannot be conjugated in the plural as in the previous phases of its deployment; it is henceforth a "collective imperialism" of the "triad" (United States, Europe and Japan). In this way, the common interests of the oligopolies which have their roots within the triad triumph over ("mercantile") conflicts of interests that may oppose them. This collective character of imperialism can be seen through the control of the global system by common instruments of the triad; at the economic level the WTO (Colonial Ministry of the triad), the IMF (Colonial Agency of collective monetary management), the World Bank (Ministry of propaganda), OECD and the European Union (set up to prevent Europe from coming out of liberalism); at the political level, the

G7, the armed forces of the United States and their subordinate instrument represented by NATO (the marginalisation/domestication of the UN completes the picture). The deployment of the project of United States' hegemony through the military control of the planet (involving among other things, the abrogation of International Law and the right that Washington has assigned itself to carry out "preventive wars" where it chooses), centres around collective imperialism and gives the North American leader the means of overcompensating for its economic deficiencies.

Objectives and means of a strategy to develop convergence in diversity

The people of the three continents (Asia, Africa and Latin America) are today faced with the expansion project of the imperialist system described as a globalised neo-liberal system which is nothing but the development of "apartheid at the global level". Will the new imperialist order in place be challenged in future? Who can challenge it? And what will be the outcome of such a challenge?

Does the image of the dominant reality not give room for the idea of an immediate challenge to this order? The ruling classes of the defeated countries of the South have largely accepted their positions as subordinate compradors; the people, helpless and fighting for daily survival, usually tend to accept their fate or even—worse—nurture new illusions which these same ruling classes shower on them (Political Islam is the most dramatic example). However, from another angle, the rise of resistant movements and the fight against capitalism and imperialism, the successes recorded—up to their electoral terms—by the new leftist governments in Latin America and Nepal (whatever the limits of the victories), the progressive radicalisation of many of these movements, and the critical positions taken by governments of the South within the WTO, are proof that "another world", a better one for that matter, is possible. The offensive strategy necessary for the reconstitution of the peoples of the South's front requires the radicalisation of social resistance in the face of capitalism's imperialist offensive.

The governing classes in some countries of the South have visibly opted for a strategy that is neither one of passive submission to the dominant forces in the global system nor one of declared opposition: a strategy of active interventions where they base their hopes in order to accelerate the development of their country. Through the solidarity of national construction produced by its revolution and Maoism, the choice to preserve the control of its currency and capital flow, the refusal to challenge the collective ownership of land (the main revolutionary gain of the peasants), China was better equipped than others to positively exploit this option and to draw unquestionably brilliant results. Can this experience be followed elsewhere? And what are some of the possible shortcomings? An analysis of the contradictions purported by this option has pushed me to conclude that the project for a national capitalism capable of asserting itself like that of the dominant powers of the global system is very much an illusion. The objective conditions inherited from history do not enable the implementation of a historic social compromise of capital/labour/rural population which will guarantee the stability of the system which, for this reason, can be directed to the right (and be confronted to growing social movements of popular classes) or evolve towards the left by constructing "market socialism" as a stage in the long transition to socialism. The apparently similar options formulated by the governing classes of other "emerging" countries are still very fragile. Neither Brazil nor India—because they did not experience radical revolutions as in China—are able to efficiently resist the combined pressures of imperialism and reactionary local classes.

Meanwhile, the nations of the South—at least some of them—now have the means that can enable them to reduce to nought the "monopoly" of technology of imperialist countries. Such nations are capable of developing themselves, without falling into the dependence trap. They have a technological mastery potential that can enable them to be able to use their own resources for themselves. They can also compel the North, by recuperating the usage of their natural resources, to adjust to a less harmful consumption method. They can equally come out of financial globalisation. They have already started challenging the monopoly of the weapons of mass destruction that the United States is planning to conserve. They can develop South-South exchange—of goods, services, capital and technology—which could not be imagined in 1955 when all these countries were deprived of industries and the mastery of technology. More than ever before, delinking from imperialism is on the agenda of possibility.

Can these nations achieve this? And who will do it? The governing bourgeoisie classes in place? I strongly doubt it. The popular classes who have come to power? This could probably begin with transitional regimes of national/popular natures.

The agrarian question is at the centre of problems to be resolved and this constitutes the main area of the national issue. The capitalist option of the private appropriation of land by a minority and the exclusion of others is entirely a borrowed option from Europe. But this was only feasible thanks to the possibility of the massive emigration of the rural population. Capitalism is unable to resolve the peasant problem of the peripheries that contain half the population of humanity in the same way. In order for these countries to succeed in their objectives, they need to have four Americas for their emigration! The alternative is the peasant system based on the access to land for all peasants. In fact the possibility of progress on this basis is potentially higher to those of the capitalist system. If we could divide the growth in productivity of modern farmers, who are few, amongst the millions of excluded people who have today become "useless", it would be more modest than we imagine. The peasant system is one of a "socialist orientation" development, to quote the Chinese and Vietnamese formula; superior and the sole guarantor of the solidarity of national construction. I will hereby refer to my article on "the Land Tenure Reforms in Asia and Africa". (ref: *Ending the crisis of capitalism or ending capitalism in crisis*?, chapter5).

National states: what is the way forward today?

According to most of what is said today, national states can no longer be the place for the definition of major choices that dictate the evolution of the economic, social and even political life of communities due to "globalization" which is a product of the expansion of the modern economy. There can therefore be no alternative, as Mrs Thatcher used to say. In reality, there are always other alternatives which by their nature can define the action margin of the National state within the global system.

There is no "law of capitalist expansion" which serves as a supernatural force. There is equally no previous historical determining factor to thisinherent trends in the logic of capitalism are challenged by resistance forces that do not accept its effects. Real history is a product of this conflict between the logic of capitalism's expansion and the social struggles of its victims against the effects of this expansion.

The effective response to the challenges facing communities can only be found if one understands that history is not determined by the infallible deployment of the laws of "pure" economy. It is produced by social reactions to trends expressed by these laws, which on their part define all social relationships within the framework in which these laws operate. "Anti-systemic forces"—if one could as such qualify this organised, coherent and effective refusal of the unilateral and total subjection to the demands of these so-called laws (in fact simply the law of private profit which characterises capitalism as a system)—shape real history as much as the "pure" logic of capitalist accumulation. They dictate possibilities and forms of expansion which are then deployed in the areas which they organise. The future is fashioned through transformations in the relationship of social and political forces; produced on their part by struggles whose outcomes are not known in advance. This however deserves some reflection, so as to contribute to the crystallisation of coherent and possible projects, while at the same time, helping social movements to overcome the "dummy solutions" where in the absence of this one, there is a risk of getting bogged down.

There are of course various interests and visions of the social and political forces under consideration expressed through different spoke-persons. These can be, as presently, the unilateral spokes-persons for the interests of the dominant trans-nationalisation of capitalism (in countries within the imperialist triad) or its subordinate "comprador" allies (in countries within the periphery). In this situation, the role of most countries has been reduced to the maintenance of internal order, while the superpower (the United States) solely exerts the responsibilities of a type of a "pseudo-world state". The United States thus alone disposes of a greater margin of autonomy while the others have nothing.

Apparently, the development of social struggles can bring to power hegemonic blocs different from those governing the globalised neo-liberal order in place, based on compromises between social interests known to be diverse and divergent (compromise blocs of capital-labour in capitalist countries, national-popular-democratic blocs, that is to say anti-compradors in the peripheries). In such a situation, the state has more possibilities. It is necessary to note that such evolutions can happen, for better or for worse.

I will add here that there are also "national interests" which legitimately recognise the establishment of a multi-polar world order. These "national interests" are usually voiced by ruling governments to justify their own specific options. Political experts of the "geo-political" set up at times such interests as "invariants" inherited from geography and history. This does not cancel the fact that they exist and play a role in determining the geometry of alliances and international conflicts, increasing and limiting at the same time the marginal activity of states.

The ancient world systems have always been multi-polar, even if such multi-polarity has never truly or generally been equal till date. For this reason, hegemony has always been a desired ambition of states rather than a reality. These hegemonies, even when they did exist, were always relative and temporal. Partners of the multi-polar world of the XIX century (extended till 1945) were exclusively "the major powers" during the period. Within the contemporary world of the triad, there are probably those who still cherish fond memories of this period and a return to this system of "balance of powers". This is not the multi-polarity desired by the vast majority of the planet (85 %!).

The multipolar world brought about by the Russian and Chinese revolutions, and later dictated partially by the liberation movements in Asia and Africa, was of a different nature. I am not hereby analysing the period after the Second World War in the conventional terms of the "bipolarity" and of the "Cold War" which does not give the progress of the countries of the South during the period the respect it deserves. I am rather analysing this multi-polarity within the terms of the conflict of basic civilization which, beyond distorting ideological expressions, deals with the conflict between capitalism and the possibility of its being eroded by socialism. The ambition of the people of the peripheries whether they staged a socialist revolution or not—to abolish the effects of polarization produced by capitalist expansion falls within an anti-capitalist perspective.

Multi-polarity is thus synonymous with the real autonomy margin of states. This margin will be used in a given manner as defined by the social content of the state in question. The Bandung period (1955-1975) in this way enabled countries of Asia and Africa to forge new ways which I have described as auto-centred development and delinking, coherent with the national-populist project of powers resulting from national liberation. There is certainly a link between the "internal" conditions defined by the national social liberation alliance at the root of the specific project of the country concerned, and the favourable external conditions (the East-West conflict was neutralising the aggressiveness of imperialism). I speak here of autonomy which is by definition relative independence, whose shortcomings are jointly determined by the nature of the national project and by the authorized action margin within the global system. This is because it remains very present and oppressive (globalization is not a strange thing!). For this reason, there is a tendency in schools of International Political Economy and of Global-Economy to challenge the importance of this action margin, and reduce it to nought. This indicates that within the globalization system (of all times) the "total" determines the "parts". I prefer an analysis in terms of complementarity/conflictuality which resituates all the powers in relation to the autonomy of national and international social and political struggles.

The aftermath of the war (1945-1980) is now history. The collective imperialist project within the triad is currently being deployed (United States, Europe, Japan) with the hegemony of the United States, which abolishes the autonomy of the countries of the South and greatly reduces those of countries associated with Washington within the imperialist triad.

The current moment is characterised by the deployment of a North American hegemony project at the international level. This project is the only one that occupies the centre stage today. There is no longer a counter project to limit the areas subjected to the control of the United States as was the case during the bipolar period (1945-1990); beyond its original ambiguities, the European project itself is fading out; countries of the South (the group of 77, the Non-Aligned) which had the ambition during the Bandung period (1955-1975) to mount a common front against western imperialism have renounced it; China itself, currently acting alone, is only interested in protecting its national project (itself ambiguous) and does not make itself an active partner of the transformation process of the world.

The collective imperialism of the triad is the result of a real evolution of the production system of capitalist countries which has not produced the emergence of a "trans-nationalised" capitalism (as the work of Hardt and Negri tends to claim), but the solidarity of the national oligopolies of countries of the system expressed in their desire to "jointly control" the world for their own self interests and profit. But if "the economy" (understood as the unilateral expression of the demands of the dominant segments of capitalism) brings together countries within the triad, politics divides their nations. The deployment of social struggles can thus challenge the role the state plays at the exclusive service of huge capital in Europe in particular. Within this hypothesis, one would expect once more to see the emergence of a polycentrism granting Europe a considerable margin of autonomy. But the deployment of "the European project" does not fall within this framework, needed to bring Washington back to reason. This project is nothing but "a European wing of the American project". The "setting up" project is one of a Europe that is implanted in its double neo-liberal and atlanticist options. The potential advanced by the conflict of political cultures, effectively requesting the end to atlanticism, remains undermined by the options of a vast majority of the left wing (in electoral terms the European socialist parties), rallied behind social-liberalism. These terms are in themselves contradictory given that liberalism is in itself non-social or even anti-social if not reactionary.

China and Russia are the two major strategic opponents of the Washington project. The ruling governments in these three countries are becoming more and more conscious of this. But they give the impression that they can operate without directly hurting the administration of the United States or even "tapping into the friendship of the United States" in conflicts opposing them to one state or the other. The "common front against terrorism"—which they all tend to adhere to—undermines things. The double game of Washington is clearly visible here: the United States on the one hand, supports the Tchetchens, Ouigurs and Tibetans just as they support Islamist movements in Algeria, Egypt, Syria and elsewhere! and on the other hand, it waves the flag of Islamist terrorism in order to rally Moscow, Beijing and Delhi behind it.

Can countries of the South play an active role in the desired defeat of the military projects and ambitions of the United States? The people attacked are presently the only active opponents capable of curbing the ambitions of Washington. Even then—and partially by the fact that they are active and feel it—the methods used in their fight remain of questionable efficiency and appeals to means which will delay the crystallisation of the solidarity of people of the North in their genuine fight. On the other hand, the analysis I have made of the "generalised compradorisation" of dominant classes and authorities in all the regions of the South leaves us with the conclusion that there are no great things to be achieved from ruling governments or those likely to be in place in the nearest future, even if they are of course "fundamentalists" (Islamists, Hindus or ethnic groups). These governments are certainly shaken at the same time by the unending arrogance of Washington and worried by the hostility (not to say hatred) of their peoples towards the United Sates. Is there anything they can really do other than to accept their fate?

For the time being, the South in general no longer has its own project as was the case during the Bandung era (1955-1975). No doubt, the ruling classes of countries qualified as "emerging" (China, India, Korea, South East Asia, Brazil and some others) have objectives they have set for themselves and which their countries are working to achieve. The objectives can be summarised as the maximization of growth within the globalisation system. These countries have—or believe themselves to have—a negotiation power that will enable them to benefit more from this "selfish" strategy than from a vague "common front" established with countries weaker than them. But the advantages they could get from this situation are specific to particular domains they are interested in and do not oppose the general structure of the system. They are thus not an alternative and do not make of this vague project (an illusion) of the construction of "national capitalism", a consistency that defines a real community project. The most vulnerable countries of the South (the "Fourth World"), do not even have their own similar projects, and the eventual product of "substitution" (religious or ethnic fundamentalism), does not merit to be qualified as such. Moreover, it is the North that solely takes the initiative to set up "for them" (one ought to say "against them") their own projects, like the European Union—ACP association (and "economic partnership agreements" called upon to replace the Cotonou Agreements with African, Caribbean and Pacific countries), the "European-Mediterranean dialogue", or the American-Israeli projects in the Middle East and even the "Greater Middle East".

The challenges facing the establishment of a reliable multipolar world are more serious than could be imagined by many "anti-globalization" movements. They are considerably many. For the time being, there is great need to rout Washington's military project. This is an indispensable condition to open up the much needed freedom margins without which any social and democratic progress and any progress towards a multipolar construction will remain very vulnerable. Given its inordinate nature, the United States' project will no doubt collapse, but certainly at a terrible human price. The resistance of its victims—people of the South—will go a long way and will be strengthened as Americans will continue to be bogged down in the numerous wars they will be compelled to be involved in. Such resistance will end up defeating the enemy and perhaps awaken opinions in the United States, as was the case with the Vietnam War. It would however be better to stop the catastrophe sooner; a situation international diplomacy can do, especially if Europe takes its responsibility as a major player seriously.

In a much longer term, "another globalization" will mean challenging the options of liberal capitalism and the management of issues of the planet through the collective imperialism of the triad within the framework of extreme Atlanticism or of its "readjusted" version. A reliable multi polar world will only become a reality when the following four conditions must have been fulfilled:

1. Europe should truly embrace the social path of "another Europe" (and thus be committed to the long transition to global socialism) and should start dissociating from its imperialist past and present. This is obviously more than simply coming out of Atlanticism and extreme neo-liberalism. Indeed there is a variety of bourgeois nationalist, fascist and social imperialist reactions to neo-liberalism that are more in line with the underlying class forces in European societies than socialist internationalism.

2. In China, "market socialism" should triumph over strong trends of the illusory construction of "national capitalism" which will be impossible to stabilise as it excludes the majority of workers and the rural population.

3. Countries of the South (people and states) should be able to build a "common front", which will enable movement margins of popular social classes not only to impose "concessions" in their favour, but also to transform the nature of the ruling governments, replacing dominant comprador blocs with "national, popular and democratic" ones.

4. At the level of the re-organisation of the systems of national and international rights, there should be progress both in the respect for national sovereignty (by moving from the sovereignty of nations to that of the people) and individual, collective, political and social rights.

Towards a revival of the bandung spirit and the reconstruction of a front of non-aligned countries on globalisation

The first wave of revival among the states and nations of Asia and Africa, which shaped major changes in the history of humankind, organised itself in the Bandung spirit in the framework of countries who were not aligned on colonialism and neo-colonialism, the pattern of globalisation at that time. This fast first assessment of Bandung does not exclude a critical analysis of the variety of visions of the countries involved with respect to their relations of subordination to western imperialism. Now, the same nations, together with those of Latin America and the Caribbean, are challenged by neoliberal globalisation, which is no less imbalanced by nature. Therefore they must unite to face the challenge successfully, as they did in the past. They will, in that perspective, feed a new wave of revival and progress on the three continents.

NAM united only the nations of Asia and Africa. The states of Latin America, with the exception of Cuba, abstained from joining the organisation. Reasons for that failure have been recorded: 1) Latin American countries were formally independent since the beginning of the nineteenth century and did not share the struggles of Asian and African nations to re-conquer their sovereignty; 2) US domination of the continent through the Monroe Doctrine was not challenged by any of the state powers in office (except Cuba—the Organisation of American States included the 'master' [the US] and was qualified for that reason by Cuba as 'the Ministry of colonies of the US'); 3) the ruling classes of European origin looked at Europe and the US as models to be copied. For those reasons, the attempt to build a 'tricontinental' consensus did not succeed; the Bandung movement was joined only by movements of struggle (often armed struggle) and was rejected by all state powers on the continent at that time.

Things have changed: 1) the countries of Latin America and the Caribbean have recently established their own organisation (CELAC, the Community of Latin American and Caribbean States), excluding the US and Canada, and have therefore formally rejected the Monroe Doctrine; 2) new popular movements have created a consciousness of the plurinational character of their societies (people having Native American, European, and African ancestors); 3) these movements have also initiated strategies of liberation from the yoke of neoliberalism, with some success, that may surpass in some respects what has been achieved elsewhere in the South. Therefore the revival of NAM must now include them and so become a tricontinental front. The axis around which the states and nations of the three continents should organise their solidarity in struggle can be formulated as building a common front against unbalanced, neoliberal, imperialist globalisation.

We have seen that the states that met in the context of Bandung held different views with respect to the ways and means of defeating imperialist domination and advancing the construction of their societies; yet they were able to overcome those differences in order to successfully face the common challenge. The same is true today. The ruling powers on the three continents as well as popular movements of struggle differ to a wide extent when it comes to the preferred ways and means to face the renewed (but essentially the same) challenges.

In some countries, 'sovereign' projects have been developed, which associate active state policies aimed at systematically constructing a consistent, national, integrated, modern industrial system of production, supported by an aggressive export capacity. Views with respect to the degree, format, and eventual regulation of opening to foreign capital and financial flows of all kinds (foreign direct investments, portfolio investments, and speculative financial investments) differ from country to country and from time to time. Policies pursued with respect to access to land and other natural resources also reflect a wide spectrum of different choices and priorities.

We find similar differences in the programmes and actions of popular movements of struggle against the official systems of power. Their priorities cover a wide spectrum: democratic rights, social rights, ecological care, gender, economic policies, access to land, and more. In a few cases, attempts have been made to bring these different demands together into a common strategic plan of action. In most cases, little has been achieved in that perspective.

Such a wide variety of situations and attitudes creates problems for all, and may even generate conflicts between states and/or between partners in struggle. So what can be done?

Sovereign projects in the perspective of a negotiated globalisation

A national sovereign project implies the concept and implementation of a set of consistent national policies aimed at 'walking on two legs': 1) constructing an integrated, auto-centred industrial system of production; 2) moving towards policies to revive and modernize peasant agriculture; and 3) articulating these two goals into a consistent, comprehensive plan of action.

Constructing an integrated, comprehensive industrial system of production implies that each industry is conceived in order to become a major provider of inputs and/or a major outlet for other industries. That concept conflicts with neoliberal dogma, which is based on the exclusive criterion of profitability for each industrial establishment considered separately from others. This concept has lead to the dismantling of some industrial systems constructed previously (in the former Soviet Union, Eastern Europe, and some countries of the global South) and to subordinating what remains of them to the status of sub-contractors for the further global expansion of giant transnational corporations (operated by financial capital from the US, some Western European countries, and Japan). My alternative concept implies state intervention—that is, state planning, managing an independent national financial system with a view to prioritising finance for the construction of industries in the framework of budget constraints to avoid inflation and the growth of foreign debt. Systems of taxation should be conceived in order to support the deployment of this project. Eventually, foreign direct investments should be required to negotiate conditions that reinforce the national project rather than annihilating it.

Defining policies aimed at reviving peasant agriculture should reduce migration out of rural areas at rates that do not allow these populations to be absorbed by urban industrial development. This target implies that land is not considered as 'merchandise', but as a common national good at the disposal of the whole population. It therefore implies ownership patterns that protect access to land for all peasant families, on as equal a footing as possible. Another target is to ensure national food sovereignty. This vision again conflicts with neoliberal dogmas and policies of so-called agricultural development based on the massive dispossession of peasants to the benefit of agribusiness, large landowners, and a minority of rich peasants. A number of priority industries should support the modernization of peasant agriculture by providing requested inputs and offering goods for consumption. Such plans for the revival of rural life should be developed for a large majority of countries in Asia and Africa as well as in Latin America, whenever the rural population still represents a significant proportion of the total population (30 percent or more) and should be adjusted to the specificities of each national case.

The first goal of such sovereign projects should be ensuring social progress for the vast majorities of working classes and reducing inequalities. The concept of neoliberal rule of an unregulated market, which is supposed to generate social justice through the windfall effects of the expansion of markets, is undermined in practice by ongoing inequality. The second goal is to create objective, favorable conditions for the invention of participatory democracy. Electoral representative democracy has been too often associated with social disaster and consequently has already lost its credibility within wide segments of these societies. The third goal is to prepare the ground for global negotiations offering countries of the South (and the former East) chances to become active, equal partners in the reconstruction of a pattern of negotiated globalisation that resists hegemony.

Practically speaking, achieving these three goals means opening channels for a debate with citizens, trade unions, and other organizations of authentic popular civil society, resulting into a plan for state support of projects of comprehensive industrialization; and opening channels with peasant popular organizations with a view to defining a plan of action for the revival of rural peasant agriculture. These are the first concrete steps we can take towards achieving the ambitious goals set out in this chapter.

References

Amin, S: *The Implosion of Contemporary capitalism.* London: Pluto Press, 2014 chap 2 (the South); chap 3 (China); chap 4 (Europe); chap 5 (the Socialist alternative)

Amin, S: *Ending the crisis of capitalism or ending capitalism?* Oxford: Pambazuka Press, 2010. Introduction (capitalism, a parenthesis in history); chap 5 (Peasant agriculture)

Amin, S: *L'Ethnie à l'assaut des Nations.* Paris, Harmattan 1994

6.

The agrarian question, a century after October 1917

In the North: an efficient capitalist family agriculture

Modern family agriculture, dominant in Western Europe and in the United States, has clearly shown its superiority compared with other forms of agricultural production. Annual production per worker (the equivalent of 1,000 to 2,000 tons of cereal) has no equal and it has enabled a minimum proportion of the active population (about 5 per cent) to supply the whole country abundantly and even produce exportable surpluses. Modern family agriculture has also shown an exceptional capacity for absorbing innovations and much flexibility in adapting to the demand.

This agriculture does not share that specific characteristic of capitalism, its main mode of labour organisation. In the factory, the number of workers enables an advanced division of labour, which is at the origin of the leap in productivity. In the agricultural family business, labour supply is reduced to one or two individuals (the farming couple), sometimes helped by one, two or three associates or permanent labourers, but also, in certain cases, a larger number of seasonal workers (particularly for the harvesting of fruit and vegetables). Generally speaking there is not a definitively fixed division of labour, the tasks being polyvalent and variable. In this sense, family agriculture is not capitalist. However, this modern family agriculture constituted an inseparable part of the capitalist economy into which it is totally integrated.

The efficiency of the agricultural family business is due to its modern equipment. They possess 90 per cent of the tractors and other agricultural equipment in use in the world. These machines are 'bought' (often on credit) by the farmers and are therefore their 'property'. In the logic of capitalism, the farmer is both a worker and a capitalist and his income should correspond to the sum of the wages for his work and the profit from his ownership of the capital being used. But it is not so. The net income of farmers is comparable to the average wage earned in industry in the same country. The State intervention and regulation policies in Europe and in the United States, where this form of agriculture dominates, have as their declared objective the aim of ensuring (through subsidies) the equality of 'peasant' and 'worker' incomes. The profits from the capital used by farmers are therefore collected by segments of industrial and financial capital further up the food chain. In actual fact, therefore, the agricultural family unit, efficient as it is is only a sub-contractor, caught in the pincers between, upstream agro-business (which imposes selected seeds today, GMOs tomorrow), industry (which supplies the equipment and chemical products), finance (which provides the necessary credits), and downstream in the commercialisation of the supermarkets. The status of the farmer is more like that of the artisan (individual producer) who used to work in the 'putting out' system (the weaver dominated by the merchant that supplied him with the thread and sold the material produced).

'Really existing socialism' carried out various experiences in 'industrial' forms of agricultural production. The 'Marxism' underlying this option was that of Karl Kautsky who, at the end of the 19th century, had 'predicted', not the modernisation of the agricultural family business (its equipment and its specialisation) but its disappearance altogether in favour of large production units, like factories, believed to benefit from the advantages of a thoroughgoing internal division of labour. This prediction did not materialise in Europe and the United States. But the myth that it transmitted was believed in the Soviet Union.

In the South: poor peasant cultivators as part of a dominated peripheral capitalism

Peasant cultivators in the South constitute almost half of humanity—three billion human beings. The types of agriculture vary, from those that have benefited from the green revolution (fertilisers, pesticides and selected seeds) although they are not very mechanised, but their production has risen to between 100 and 500 quintals per labourer, to those which are the same as before this revolution whose production is only around 10 quintals per labourer. The gap between the average production of a farmer in the North and that of peasant agriculture, which was 10 to 1 before 1940 is now 100 to 1. In other words, the rate of progress in agricultural productivity has largely outstripped that of other activities, bringing about a lowering of the real price from 5 to 1.

This peasant agriculture in the countries of the South is also well and truly integrated into local and world capitalism. However, closer study reveals immediately both the convergences and differences in the two types of 'family' economy. There are huge differences: the importance of subsistence food in the peasant economies, the only way of survival for those rural populations; the low efficiency of this agriculture, not equipped with tractors or other materials and often highly parcellised; the poverty of the rural world (three quarters of the victims of under-nourishment are rural); the growing incapacity of these systems to ensure food supplies for their towns; the sheer immensity of the problems as the peasant economy affects nearly half of humanity. In spite of these differences, peasant agriculture is already integrated into the dominant global capitalist system. I therefore qualify these cases not as examples of "capitalist agriculture" but as those of "agriculture in capitalism".

Is the modernisation of the agriculture of the South by capitalism possible and desirable?

Let us use the hypothesis of a strategy for the development of agriculture that tries to reproduce systematically in the South the course of modern family agriculture in the North. One could easily imagine that some 50 million more modern farms, if given access to the large areas of land which would be necessary (taking it from the peasant economy and of course choosing the best soils) and if they had access to the capital markets enabling them to equip themselves, they could produce the essential of what the creditworthy urban consumers still currently obtain from peasant agriculture. But what would happen to the billions of non-competitive peasant producers? They would be inexorably eliminated in a short period of time, a few decades. What would happen to these billions of human beings, most of them already the poorest of the poor, but who feed themselves, for better and/or for worse—and for a third of them, for worse? Within a time horizon of fifty years, no industrial development, more or less competitive, even in a far-fetched hypothesis of a continual yearly growth of 7 per cent for three-quarters of humanity, could absorb even a third of this labour reserve. Capitalism, by its nature, cannot resolve the peasant question: the only prospects it can offer are a planet full of slums and billions of 'too many' human beings.

We have therefore reached the point when, to open up a new field for the expansion of capital ('the modernisation of agricultural production'), it is necessary to destroy—in human terms—entire societies. Fifty million new efficient producers (200 million human beings with their families) on the one hand, three billion of excluded people on the other. The creative aspect of the operation would be only a drop of water in the ocean of destruction that it requires. I thus conclude that capitalism has entered into its phase of declining senility: the logic of the system is no longer able to ensure the simple survival of humanity. Capitalism is becoming barbaric and leads directly to genocide.

Therefore is capitalist modernisation path as 'effective' as the conventional economists claim? Let us imagine that, in this way, we can double production (from an index of 100 to one of 200) but that this is obtained by the elimination of 80 per cent of the surplus rural population (the index of the number of active cultivators falling from 100 to 20). The apparent gain, measured by the growth of production per active producer is considerable: it is multiplied by ten. But, if it is seen in terms of the rural population as a whole, it is only multiplied by two. Therefore it is necessary to distribute freely all this growth in production in order simply to keep alive the peasants who have been eliminated and cannot find alternative work in the towns.

This was what Marx wrote concerning the pauperisation associated with the accumulation of capital.

So, what's to be done?

It is necessary to accept the maintenance of peasant agriculture for all the visible future of the 21st century. Not for reasons of romantic nostalgia for the past, but quite simply because the solution of the problem is to overtake the logics that drive capitalism and to participate in the long, secular transition to world socialism

Land tenure reform is at the heart of the choices concerning the future of peasant societies

The main issue of the debate on the future of peasant agricultures concerns the question of the rules governing the access to land.

Land tenure systems based on the private ownership of land

In this case the owner disposes of, to use the terms of Roman law, the usus (right to develop), the fructus (ownership of the products of this exploitation) and the abusus (the right to transfer ownership). This right is 'absolute' in that the owner can cultivate his land himself, he can rent it out or he can even keep it out of cultivation. Ownership can be given or sold, it is part of a collection of assets deriving from the rights of inheritance.

This land tenure system is modern in the sense that it is the result of the constitution of 'really existing' capitalism, starting from Western Europe and from the colonies of European extraction in America. It was set up through the destruction of the 'customary' systems of regulating access to the land in Europe itself. The statutes of feudal Europe were founded on the superimposing of rights on the same land: those of the peasant concerned and other members of the village community (serfs or freedmen), those of the feudal lord and those of the king. The assault on these rights took the form of the Enclosures in England, imitated in various ways in all the European countries during the 19th century. Marx very soon denounced this radical transformation that excluded most of the peasants from access to the use of land—and who were destined to become emigrant proletarians in the town or remain where they were as agricultural labourers (or sharecroppers)—and he classified these measures as primitive accumulation, dispossessing the producers of the land and the use of the means of production.

Land tenure systems not based on the private ownership of land

This definition, being negative, cannot apply to a homogenous group. For, in all human societies access to the land is regulated. But this is done either through 'customary communities'. 'modern local authorities' or the State. Or, more precisely, and more often, by a collection of institutions and practices that concern individuals, local authorities and the State.

The 'customary' management has almost always excluded private ownership and always guaranteed access to the land to all the families concerned—that is, those who constitute a distinct 'village community' and identify themselves as such. But it hardly gave 'equal' access to the land. Customary management has almost never been that of 'independent villages', which were in fact nearly always integrated into some sort of State, stable or shifting, solid or precarious, but seldom absent. The usage rights of communities and of the families that composed them have always been limited by those of the State that received tribute (which is the reason why I described the vast array of pre-modern production modes as 'tributary').

These complex kinds of 'customary management exist, at best, in extremely degraded forms, having suffered from the attack by the dominating logic of globalised capitalism for at least two centuries (in Asia and Africa) and sometimes five centuries (in Latin America). The example of India is probably the most striking in this regard. Before the British colonisation, access to land was administered by the 'village communities' or, more exactly, their governing castes, excluding the inferior castes—the dalits—who were treated as a kind of collective slave class, similar to the helots of Sparta. These communities, in turn, were controlled and exploited by the imperial Mogul State and its vassals (rajahs and other kings), who levied the taxes. The British raised the status of the zamindars (whose responsibility it was to actually collect the taxes) to becoming 'owners', so that they constituted a kind of allied large land-owning class, regardless of tradition. On the other hand, they maintained the 'tradition' when it suited them, for example excluding the dalits from access to land! Independent India did not challenge this heavy colonial inheritance, which is the cause of the unbelievable destitution of most of the peasantry and thus of its urban population (see 'India a Great Power?' in Samir Amin, Beyond US Hegemony—see references below).

As a result, the private ownership of land is now applicable to most agricultural land—particularly the most fertile ones—in all Asia, except for China, Vietnam and the former Soviet republics of Central Asia. There remain only the vestiges of para-customary systems, particularly in the poorest areas and those less attractive to prevailing capitalist agriculture. This structure is highly differentiated, juxtaposing large landowners (rural capitalists in my terminology), rich peasants, middle peasants, poor peasants without land. There is no peasant organization or movement that transcends these acute class conflicts.

China and Vietnam provide a unique example of a system for managing access to the land which is neither based on private ownership, nor on 'custom', but on a new revolutionary right, unknown elsewhere, which is that of all the peasants (described as the inhabitants of a village) having equal access to land (and I stress the 'equal'). This is the most beautiful acquisition of the Chinese and Vietnamese revolutions. Mao Zedong is the first—and no doubt the only, followed by Chinese and Vietnamese communists—to have prescribed an agrarian revolution strategy based on the mobilization of most of the poor peasants, without land or other assets. The victory of this revolution made it possible to abolish the private ownership of land right from the beginning—which was replaced by that of the State—as well as the organisation of new forms of equal access to land for all peasants. True, this procedure has passed through several successive stages, including the Soviet-inspired model based on production cooperatives. The limits of their achievements led both countries to return to the idea of family peasant units. Are they viable? Can they produce a continual improvement in production without freeing up too much rural labour? On what conditions? What kinds of support are required from the State? What forms of political management can meet this challenge?

Ideally, the model involves the double affirmation of the rights of the State (the only owner) and of the usufructuaries (the peasant family). The State guarantees the equal division of the village lands among all the families and it prohibits all other usage other than family cultivation, for example, the renting of land. It guarantees that the result of investments made by the usufructuaries are given back to them immediately through their right of ownership of all the produce of their land, which are marketed freely, although the State guarantees purchase at a minimum price. On the longer term the children who remain on the land can inherit from the usufructuaries (those who definitively leave the place lose their right to the land, which reverts to the lands for future redistribution). This is the case, of course, for fertile land, but also for the small, even dwarf-sized plots, so that the system is only viable if there is vertical investment (the green revolution without much mechanisation), which proves as effective in increasing production through rural activities as horizontal investment (extension of the holdings, supported by intensified mechanisation).

Not only one formula for peasant alternatives

'Agrarian reform' should be understood as the redistribution of private ownership when it is considered to be unequally distributed. It is a land tenure system that is based on the principle of ownership. This reform becomes necessary both to satisfy the demand (perfectly legitimate) from poor and landless peasants and to reduce the political and social power of the large landowners. But where it is implemented, in Asia and Africa after the liberation of old forms of imperialist and colonial domination, it has been carried out by hegemonic non-revolutionary social blocs who were not governed by the dominated and poor majority classes. The exceptions were in China and Vietnam where, also for this reason, there had not been an 'agrarian reform' in the strict sense of the term but, as I have said, private ownership of land was suppressed, the principle of State ownership was affirmed and the 'equal' access to the use of land by all the peasants was put into operation. Elsewhere, real reforms only dispossessed the large landowners to the profit, finally, of the middle and even rich (long-term) peasants, ignoring the interests of the poor and those without land. That was the case in Egypt and in other Arab countries. The reform under way in Zimbabwe risks ending up in the same way. In other situations, reform is always on the agenda of what should be done: in India, in South-East Asia, in South Africa and in Kenya.

The progress created by agrarian reform, even where it exists as an immediate and essential requirement, is nevertheless ambiguous for its more long-term implications. For it reinforces attachment to 'small property' which becomes an obstacle to the questioning of a land tenure system based on private ownership.

Russia's history illustrates this drama. The developments that followed the abolition of serfdom, which took place in 1861, which were accelerated by the revolution of 1905 because Stolypin's policies had already produced a 'claim for ownership' that was (finally) fulfilled in the radical agrarian reform after the 1917 revolution. And, as we know, the new small owners did not enthusiastically renounce their rights for the benefit of the unfortunate cooperatives, which were dreamt up at the time, in the 1930s. 'Another path' to development, based on the peasant family economy of the generalized small owners, would have been possible. But it was not attempted.

Here we find the old debate. Towards the end of the 19th century, Marx, in his correspondence with the Russian Narodniks (Vera Zasulich, among others), dared to say that the absence of private ownership could constitute an advantage for the socialist revolution, enabling a leap forward towards a regime for managing the access to land other than the one governed by private ownership. But he did not specify what forms this new regime should take, the adjective 'collective', correct as it was, being insufficient. Twenty years later Lenin believed this possibility no longer existed, eliminated by the penetration of capitalism and the spirit of private ownership that accompanied it. Was this a correct assessment? I cannot say, as I do not know enough about Russia. However, Lenin was hardly able to give decisive importance to this question, having accepted the viewpoint of Kautsky in The Agrarian Question.

The question came up again in the 1960s, when Africa attained its independence. The national liberation movements of the continents, the States and the State-Parties which it had produced received, in different degrees, the support of the peasant majorities of their peoples. Their natural tendency to populism was to imagine a "specific ('African') path to socialism". This could be described as very moderately radical in its relationships both with dominant capitalism and with the local classes associated with its expansion. Nevertheless it posed the question of reconstruction of peasant society in a humanist and universalist spirit. This spirit was often very critical of 'traditions' that the foreign masters had in fact been trying to mobilise for their own profit.

What the dominant discourse at the moment means by 'reform of the land tenure system' is the exact opposite of what is required for the building of an authentic alternative based on a prosperous peasant economy. What this discourse, conveyed by the propaganda instruments of collective imperialism—the World Bank, many development institutions, but also a number of NGOs that are richly endowed—means by land reform is the acceleration of the privatisation of land, and nothing more. The aim is clear: to create the conditions that would enable some 'modern' islands of agrobusiness (foreign and local) to take over the land they require to expand. But the supplementary produce that these 'islands' could supply (for export or for local 'effective demand') could never meet the needs for building a prosperous society for all, which would involve the development of the peasant family economy as a whole.

Need to define role of the State in land reform

We refer the reader to the writings of Jacques Berthelot on these questions. He is the best and most critical analyst of the projects to integrate agricultural and food production into the 'world' markets. We shall just mention the conclusions and most important proposals that we have reached. It is not possible to accept that agricultural and food production, as well as land be treated as ordinary 'goods' and thus allow them to be integrated into the project of globalized liberalization promoted by the dominant powers and trans nationalised capital. The WTO agenda must be rejected.

The alternative consists of national policies to construct/reconstruct national funds for stabilization and support for production, completed by the establishment of common international funds for basic products, enabling an effective alternative reorganization of the international markets of agricultural products.

The peasants of Asia and Africa organized themselves during the stage prior to the liberation struggles of their peoples. They found their place in the strong historical blocs which made it possible to win victory over the imperialism of the time. These blocs were sometimes revolutionary (China and Vietnam) and they then had their main rural bases in the majority classes of middle peasants and poor, landless peasants. Or, elsewhere, they were led by the national bourgeoisie or sectors who aspired to become so among the rich and middle peasants, thus isolating the large landowners in some places and the 'customary' chieftainries in the pay of the colonisers.

That page of history having been turned, the challenge of the new collective imperialism of the Triad (United States, Europe and Japan) will only be got rid of if historical blocs are constituted in Asia and Africa. But this cannot be a remake of the preceding blocs. The challenge faced by the so-called alternative world movement and its constitutive components of social forums is to identify, in the new conditions, the nature of these blocs, their strategies and immediate and long-term objectives. This is a far more serious challenge than is realized by many of the movements committed to the struggles.

The challenge, which is to base development on renewing peasant societies, has many dimensions. I will just call attention here to the conditions for constructing the necessary and possible political alliances that will enable progress to be made towards solutions (in the interests of the worker peasants, of course) to all the problems that are posed: access to the land and to the means to develop it properly: reasonable wages for peasant work, improvement of wages parallel to the productivity of this work, appropriate regulation of the markets at the national, regional and world levels.

I myself am not so naïve as to think that all the interests that these alliances represent can naturally converge. In all peasant societies there are the rich and the poor (who are often without land). The conditions of access to land result from different historical experiences which, in some, have rooted aspirations to ownership in peoples' minds while in others, it is to protect the access to land of the greatest number. The relationships of the peasantries to State power are also the result of different political paths, particularly as concerns the national liberation movements of Asia and Africa: populisms, peasant democracies, State anti-peasant autocracies show the diversity of peoples' heritages. The way in which international markets are run favour some, penalise others. These divergences of interest are sometimes echoed in many of the peasant movements and often in the divergences of the political strategies adopted.

References

Alternatives Agroécologiques & Solidaires: https://www.sol-asso.fr/analyses-politiques-agricoles-jacques-b-2/ (accessed 3 September 2017)

Amin, S (ed): *Les luttes paysannes et ouvrières face aux défis du xxie siècle – L'avenir des sociétés paysannes et la reconstruction du front uni des travailleurs.* Paris: Les Indes Savantes 2005. Includes references to peasant struggles in China, India, Philippines, Sri Lanka, Egypt, Ethiopia, West Africa, South Africa and Zimbabwe.

Amin, S: 'L'Inde, une grande puissance?' in Samir Amin: *Pour un monde multipolaire.* Paris: Editions Syllepse 2005. Chapter 4, London: Zed Books, 2006

Berthelot, J: *L'agriculture : talon d'Achille de la mondialisation : clés pour un accord agricole solidaire à l'OMC.* Paris: Harmattan 2001

Chayanov, A: 'On the Theory of Non-Capitalist economic systems' in *The Theory of Peasant Economy*, (eds. Thorner, Kerblay y Smith), 1966, págs.1-28. 1966

Kautsky, K. *The Agrarian Question*, Vol I. London: Zwan Publications. 1988(first German edition 1899)

Mamdani, M: *Citizen and Subject: Contemporary Africa and the Legacy of Late Colonialism,* New Jersey: Princeton University Press 1996

Mafeje, A: *The Agrarian Question Access to Land and Peasant Responses in Sub-Saharan Africa*, Geneva: UNRISD, 2003

Mazoyer, M and Roudard, L: *Histoire des agricultures du monde*, Paris: Seuil, 1997

Moyo, S: Land in the Political Economy of African Development: Alternative Strategies for Reform. Africa Development, Vol. 32 (4) 2007, pp. 1–34 CODESRIA

Parmentier, B: *Nourrir l'humanité*, Paris: La Découvert, 2007

Shivji, I: 'Relfections'. Interviewd by Marc Wuyts. *Development and Change*. 39(6): 1079-1090. Institute of Social Studies, 2008

www.ingramcontent.com/pod-product-compliance
Lightning Source LLC
Chambersburg PA
CBHW070149080526
44586CB00015B/1905